Oregon's Coast

OREGON'S COAST

A Guide to the Best Family Attractions from Astoria to Brookings

David and Carolyn Gabbe

JASI

Johnston Associates International
P.O. Box 313, Medina, WA 98039

ISBN: 1-881409-00-7

The listings and information appearing in this edition were current at the
time of the final editing, but are subject to change at any time. No
gratuities of any kind have been solicited or accepted from listed firms.

First Printing May, 1992
Cover art and book design by Mike Jaynes
Production by Lasergraphics

JASI
Post Office Box 313
Medina, Washington 98039 U.S.A.
(206) 454–7333

Printed in the United States of America
Distributed in Canada by Raincoast Books Ltd.

Acknowledgements

Our first thanks must go to our publisher who saw the promise for an Oregon Coast family travel guide and gave us the opportunity to write it. In addition, we gratefully acknowledge the assistance of state and local tourism offices, chambers of commerce, park rangers, museum curators, interpretive center personnel, and scores of fellow family travelers and others who shared their experiences and "secrets" with us. Especially helpful were Monte Turner, Oregon Parks and Recreation Department; Ranotta McNair and Marilyn Krause, Oregon Dunes National Recreation Area; Lynn Wallace, Astoria Area Chamber of Commerce; Jesse Greco, Coos Bay/North Bend Convention Bureau; Carol Posey, Depoe Bay Chamber of Commerce; Rebecca Ruede, Florence Area Chamber of Commerce; Loriann Sheridan, Lincoln City Chamber of Commerce; Jacque Potter, Lower Umpqua Chamber of Commerce; Phil Hutchinson, Greater Newport Chamber of Commerce; Ruth Daugherty, Rockaway Chamber of Commerce; Joyce Stewart, Seaside Chamber of Commerce; Robbie Schoonover, Yachats Chamber of Commerce; Mike Rivers, Alsea Bay Interpretive Center; Norma Jean Bice, Lincoln City Recreation Department; Dennis Strayer, Siskiyou National Forest; Bandon Chamber of Commerce; Bay Area Chamber of Commerce; Brookings-Harbor Chamber of Commerce; Cannon Beach Chamber of Commerce; Charleston Visitors Information Center; Garibaldi Chamber of Commerce; Gold Beach Chamber of Commerce; Nehalem Bay Area Chamber of Commerce; North Bend Information Center; Pacific City Woods Chamber of Commerce; Port Orford Chamber of Commerce; Tillamook Chamber of Commerce; and Waldport Chamber of Commerce.

Finally, many thanks to our young traveling companions, C.J. and Wendy Gabbe, for being such good-natured subjects and for enabling us to see the Oregon Coast's attractions through the fresh eyes of children.

Introduction

Oregon's magnificent coast has it all: 362 miles of rugged coastline dotted with picturesque towns, parks, beaches, landmarks, museums, and attractions of all kinds. It's a vast, wondrous playground for adults and children to explore and enjoy. *Oregon's Coast: A Guide To The Best Family Attractions from Astoria to Brookings* is our effort to make family travel to the Oregon Coast a memorable event. We've compiled a listing of places—from parks and playgrounds to museums and festivals—geared especially to the visitor travelling with children of all ages. Of course, most grown-ups will have just as good a time as the kids. We've selected activities because of their appeal to the child in each of us.

We've traveled with our children ever since they were very young and have come to believe that the best family trips were those that included lots of attractions that all of us enjoyed visiting.

Some of the best adventures on the Oregon Coast may require only an hour or two of your time, while others will easily fill up a half-day or more. We've included admission prices, hours, and phone numbers, wherever possible. But don't forget: prices and hours are always subject to change; if the cost of entrance is important, it's best to call ahead.

As you'll experience for yourself, it's really not necessary to spend a lot of money to have a good time exploring this natural playground. Some of the most enchanting and delightful hours with your family can be spent at the many free attractions included in this book.

Although it does take some thinking and planning on your part when considering the needs of younger travelers, it's been our intent in researching this guidebook to make your family travel easier and more enjoyable.

We're sure your visit to the Oregon Coast will be one to remember joyfully—provided you and your family heed some basic safety rules for the coast areas. Here are a few recommendations that may help to insure that your trip is a comfortable, enjoyable, and safe one.

- Try not to turn your back to the ocean, especially in winter when the waves are larger and stronger and can easily knock a person off his feet. More importantly, be alert at all times for so-called sneaker waves—unusually large waves that are particularly dangerous to children. Sneaker waves have been known to cause fatalities. Often caught by surprise, children or even adults are quickly carried out to see by the undertow. Remember: Don't turn your back to the ocean!
- Never allow children to play on or even around logs and driftwood. Not only can they contain nails, broken glass, and other snags, they are easily moved and rolled by the action of the surf. Many people have suffered bone fractures and other serious, crippling injuries under the crush of rolling logs in the surf.
- Always be aware of the tides. Check them before you go on the beach, rocks, or in the water. Tide cards are available at most motels, sporting goods stores, and other shops. The outgoing tide is the most hazardous for young swimmers, as it can pull youngsters—almost anything—in its path. Incoming tides pose the most risk for those fishing or exploring offshore rocks.
- When hiking and climbing, stay behind retaining walls and be sure the youngsters do, too. Cliff trails are slippery in wet weather! It's unwise to climb on beach cliffs, as the soil, rocks, and shallow-rooted shrubbery provide inadequate climbing support. Offshore rock climbing may be fun, but the rocks are often slippery and have sharp, jagged edges. Children must be careful—falls could cause serious injuries.
- Although frolicking on the sand dunes makes a great family outing, exploring the dunes alone is not for the inexperienced or for children. At times, blowing and shifting sand can quickly wipe out footprints and create a "white-out"—making it easy for you to get lost. A lot like snow, sand is very unstable and can easily collapse on

youngsters busy digging and tunneling. Occasionally, wild animals, including black bears, are present in the dunes. These animals can be dangerous and should not be approached for any reason.

- Children should never swim alone. They should swim away from heavy surf or currents and under the supervision of their parents or other adults. Since the surf can hide depressions in the sand, it's a good idea that smaller youngsters never be permitted to wade any deeper than their knees.
- Even beachcombing has its potential dangers. Besides sneaker waves, wave-tossed logs, and nails or glass found in debris, there's the possibility of a sudden encounter with motorized vehicles on beaches where they are permitted.

Please take the time to explain these dangers to your children. Although other unforeseen hazards may be lurking about, the use of common sense and obeying local safety warnings can go a long way to insure you'll always have happy memories of the Oregon Coast.

Preface

Travel guides are necessarily selective. Attractions in this book were picked for their suitability for those traveling with youngsters. Some attractions appeal to the very young, others to teenagers. We've aimed to cover the entire age range so that you can plan a successful family visit to Oregon's fabulous coastal playground.

We've done our best to put together the most accurate guide possible. Nevertheless, hours of operation, phone numbers, and admission prices are subject to change. Sometimes an attraction may be closed for renovation or repair. Accept our apologies if something has changed and please call ahead to check all places you wish to visit.

If we have omitted some of your favorite places or activities, please drop us a note at P.O. Box 5163, Eugene, Oregon 97405. Your comments would be appreciated.

Table of Contents

Section 1
North Oregon Coast

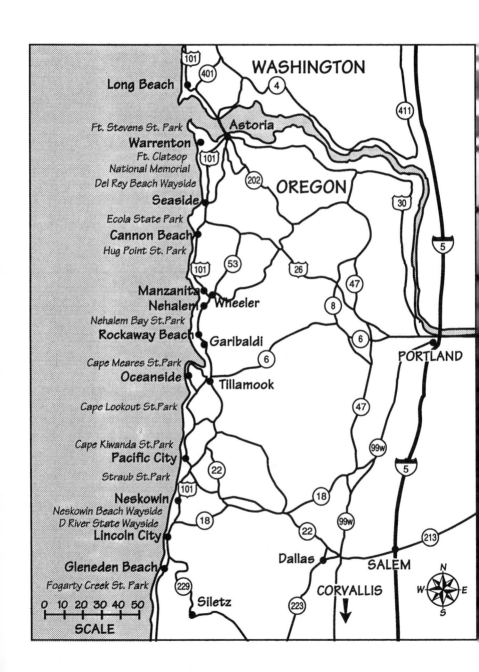

ASTORIA

O regon's history—in fact, that of the entire American West—begins in Astoria. It was in 1811 that John Jacob Astor, then America's wealthiest man, built the first U.S. settlement west of the Mississippi at Fort Astoria as a base for his burgeoning Pacific Fur Company. Although it fell briefly into the hands of the British following the War of 1812, Astoria was returned to American control and welcomed an influx of traders, explorers, missionaries, and settlers. Today, sprawling Victorians on the flanks of Coxcomb Hill, many of them restored as bed-and-breakfasts, reflect the town's prosperous early history.

Modern Astoria is a curious blend of late 19th century small American town and hard-working port city. Although endowed with historic homes and exhibits, museums, and fine recreational offerings, Astoria bears scant resemblance to a tourist town. It should be one of the West's prime tourist stops, yet strangely enough, it is often overlooked as a tourist destination.

Sights and Attractions

Astoria Column

Location: Coxcomb Hill Rd., Astoria
Phone: 325–6311
Days/Hours: Daily 9–dusk
Cost: Free

The Astoria Column, patterned after Trajan's Column in Rome, was built in 1926 by a railway company to complete a series of monuments erected along its right of way. A 166-step spiral staircase decorated with murals and words depicting Astoria's major historical events, leads to an observation deck atop this 125-foot-high tower. Even at the foot of this monolith, the view of Astoria and its waterfront over 700 feet below is quite impressive. Although the climb does require a bit of energy, children love racing to the top—and if the ascent doesn't take your breath away, the panoramic views from the circular observation deck will. Since the youngsters will be interested in knowing what they're looking at, it's best to be prepared: off to the west, the mouth of the Columbia as it empties into the ocean; to the northeast the dramatically-altered cone of Mount St. Helens, which erupted in May 1980; Youngs Bay and Saddle Mountain are visible to the south; towards the waterfront, the Astoria Bridge links Oregon and Washington.

Astoria Flight Center

Location: Astoria Airport, off Hwy 101
Phone: 861–1222
Days/Hours/Cost: Call for flight information

The Astoria Flight Center provides scenic 40-minute flights over the Columbia River and along the coast. One person is charged $40; groups of two or three people pay a total of $65. Whale-watching flights available. Special flight tours and air taxi service can be arranged by reservation only.

Astoria Waterfront

Location: End of 6th St., Astoria

The city's waterfront is a veritable beehive of activity that will fascinate every member of the family. Huge ocean-going ships, as well as commercial fishing vessels and sailboats, are regularly seen coming or going. You'll watch longshoremen at work, dwarfed by mammoth vessels, as they load logs or unload paper or other commodities. Youngsters love watching lift cranes carry immense cargo or special handling equipment moving around on the docks. Dramatic views of the spectacular Astoria Bridge are possible from your waterfront perch. This four mile long structure is thought to be the longest continuous three-span truss bridge in the world.

Columbia River Maritime Museum

Location: 1792 Marine Dr., Astoria
Phone: 325-2323
Days/Hours: Daily 9:30–5
Cost: $3/adults, $1.50/ages 6–18

The Columbia River Maritime Museum, one of America's finest, brings to life over 200 years of the rich maritime history of the Pacific Northwest. Its numerous galleries house superb displays about shipwrecks, lighthouses, exploration, fishing, and naval history. Several unique exhibits are absolutely hands-on—and children will love every moment at them. Youngsters can scramble aboard the bridge of a WWII Navy destroyer, peer through an operational submarine periscope at the busy river traffic, and enter a Columbia River sternwheeler pilot house to stand a turn at the wheel. In addition, rope-making and net-mending demonstrations are scheduled most weekends.

Be sure not to miss the Shipwreck Gallery for a sobering look at the personal belongings of some of the ill-fated passengers from the 2,000 ships that have been wrecked at the mouth of the Columbia River since the early 1800s. The admission price includes entrance to the Coast Guard Lightship Columbia moored on the river adjacent to the museum.

Flavel House

Location: 441 8th St., Astoria
Phone: 325-2203
Days/Hours: Daily 10-5 (May thru October), 11-4 (rest of year)
Cost: $3/adults, $1/ages 6-12

The Pride of Astoria is the Queen Anne Victorian mansion built by millionaire shipping tycoon George Flavel. Its decorative exterior of balconies, verandas, and three-story octagon tower testify to the opulent style of Victorian architecture. Strolling through this house is like travelling back in time to the late 19th century. On display are clothing, art and a household of furnishings reflecting the life-style of the rich and famous of another era. Youngsters are treated to a view of the toy collection in the Flavel children's room as well as by a basement full of many old machines. Fourteen-foot-high ceilings, exquisitely milled doors, winding staircases, Persian rugs, and a half-dozen fireplaces with mantels carved from different hardwoods are a few of the other features of "the house with the red roof." The admission price includes entrance to the Heritage Center Museum (see description in this chapter).

Fort Astoria

Location: 15th & Exchange Sts., Astoria
Days/Hours: Daily, dawn to dusk
Cost: Free

Upon this site in 1811 the Pacific Fur Trading Company established the first permanent American outpost west of the Mississippi. Although the fort they built has long since passed into history, a partially recreated log fort gives visitors a special feel for what the original was like. Several short lectures recounting the fort's rich historical background are given each day during summer between 11 a.m. and 3:30 p.m. A visit to this small historical park will be an enjoyable stop for the whole family, and especially for those with an interest in American history.

Fort Clatsop National Memorial

Location: Off Hwy 101, Warrenton
Phone: 861-2471
Days/Hours: Daily 8–6 (summer), 8–5 (rest of year)
Cost: $1/adults, free/under 16

Fort Clatsop National Memorial is an exact reproduction of the encampment used by the intrepid explorers Lewis and Clark during the winter of 1805. The fort's visitor center nicely recounts the famous expedition with displays, maps, artifacts, slides, and a short, but engrossing film. However, the main reason to come here is to experience their summer "living history" reenactments. Park rangers, dressed in early 19th century costumes, enact the day to day activities of the Lewis and Clark party in their struggle for survival. These incredible demonstrations will captivate the kids, especially the older ones. You'll see how the explorers tanned and sewed hides, made tallow candles, cured jerky, made lead bullets, loaded and fired muskets, made leather clothes and moccasins, and performed a number of other life-sustaining enterprises. In addition, youngsters will occasionally have a chance to help hollow out a canoe, scrape a hide, or use flint and steel to make the sparks for a fire. These demonstrations and hands-on experiences give children an excellent opportunity to understand the conditions under which Lewis and Clark survived. The park also features picnic sites and nicely landscaped trails that lead from the visitor center to the fort, to a spring, and to a canoe landing—all used by the explorers nearly 200 years ago.

Fort Stevens Historic Area

Location: On Hwy 101, Hammond
Phone: 861-2000
Days/Hours: Daily 10–6 (summer), Wed–Sun 10–4 (rest of year)
Cost: Free

The Union Army built Fort Stevens during the Civil War to keep Confederate frigates from entering the Columbia River. Although that threat never materialized, Fort Stevens underwent a massive military build-up in the decades that followed. The fort gained notoriety in 1942 when a Japanese submarine opened fire on it with its five-inch guns. The shelling caused no damage, but Fort Stevens remains the only military installation in the continental U.S. to be fired upon since the War of 1812. After World War II the fort was deactivated and turned over to the National Park Service.

Today, an interpretive center in the former War Games Building displays weapons, maps, photos of guns in action, and other relics. Children love exploring some of the massive gun batteries and climbing to the nearby commander's station to guard against enemy submarines or some Rebel man-of-war trying to slip by. In summer, special tours and "living history" events turn back the clock to the time when Fort Stevens was a sentinel on the Colombia River. A trip to an eerie subterranean gun battery will give imaginative youngsters a feel for the life of a "concrete cannoneer," as seacoast artillerymen were often called. Topside, every third weekend of the month, Union soldiers in authentic costumes can be seen manning the fort, firing cannon shot at enemy targets, and cleaning and shooting their muskets. Hopping aboard a World War II troop carrier for a dynamic tour of the fort's grounds is an unusual way to explore the past.

Heritage Center Museum

Location: 16th & Exchange Sts., Astoria
Phone: 325-2203
Days/Hours: Daily 10–5 (May thru September), 11–4 (rest of year)
Cost: $3/adults, $1/ages 6–12

Astoria's rich history is graphically depicted in several galleries that house an impressive array of tools, weapons, kitchen utensils, photos and other artifacts. The museum's two floors of exhibits are in the former City Hall, a restored neoclassical structure built around the turn of the century. Some of the exhibits include artifacts from the world famous Louvre in France, as well as items recovered from the Peter Iredale shipwreck. Kids enjoy a peek into the old jail, which was used until the mid-1970s. The thousands of artifacts and photos on display in the Heritage Center Museum provide a constantly changing glimpse into Astoria's colorful past. The admission price includes entrance to the Flavel House (see description in this chapter).

Uppertown Fire Fighters Museum

Location: 30th & Marine Dr., Astoria
Phone: 325-2203
Days/Hours: Daily 10–5 (May thru October), 11–4 (rest of year)
Cost: $3/adults, $1/ages 6–12

This stout brick building, constructed in 1896, was first a brewery and then a firehouse for 40 years. Today it is the repository of a fascinating fire fighters collection. Visitors will see a gleaming exposition of hand-pulled, horse-drawn, and motorized vehicles that were in service from 1877 to 1921. Of particular interest to children are an 1878 Hayes Ladder Wagon and a 1921 Stutz that could pump a thousand gallons per minute—quite a feat in those days. In addition, the museum features a bizarre bunch of fire extinguishers that date from the 1890s to the mid-20th century. Several funny-looking jump nets used in the 1940s and 1950s make a modern viewer wonder if many people chose instead to remain in burning buildings than chance a leap into these contraptions. Some particularly sobering photos of Astoria's major blazes round out an impressive collection with something to appeal to every member of the family.

Youngs River Falls

Location: Youngs River Loop, 8 miles south of Astoria

A short, pleasant drive off the beaten track brings visitors to some of Astoria's beautiful, verdant "backwoods." Though they are not considered one of Oregon's truly majestic water-falls, the Youngs River Falls drop 65 feet over mossy canyon walls. More than 100 years ago this was the site of a pulp mill; today it's a small county park with a short trail down a ravine to a picnic site. This is an uncrowded park that's ideal for a family picnic and a youthful romp.

Parks and Camping

Fort Stevens State Park
Location: South of Ridge Rd. from Pacific Dr., Hammond
Phone: 861–1671
Cost: Free/day use, $9–13/camping
Oregon's largest state park features a staggering 605 campsites within the confines of its 4,000 acre territory. The campground is open all year, providing a full variety of sites for recreational vehicles, campers, and tents. Two large, sheltered picnic areas are located on Coffenbury Lake, which offers fishing, boating, and two great swimming beaches. An easy nature trail around the lake makes for a great family stroll. Besides the military installations at the park's Historic Area (see description in this chapter), visitors can also view the remains of the Peter Iredale, a British schooner that shipwrecked on the park's beach nearly a century ago. On the northwest tip of the park, an observation deck atop South Jetty makes an ideal spot to watch waves breaking over the jetty and the big ships entering the Columbia.

Tapiola Park and Pool
Location: Denver St. & Marine Dr., Astoria
Phone: 325–7027
Days/Hours/Cost: Call for fees and hours (June thru August)
As spring turns into summer and the weather gets warm, many Astorians head for the nearest swimming hole. At Tapiola Park, a large outdoor swimming pool is available to help cool you off (although on one of the Oregon Coast's chilly summer days, this heated pool might just help warm you up). For young children, a small wading pool is just the place for some serious splashing while the grown-ups rest on the sidelines. Swimming lessons are available for those who have the time to learn. This park also features picnic sites and play equipment, making it an ideal family stop for a few hours.

Annual Events

Astoria Monster Bash
Location: Fairgrounds, 20th & Marine Dr., Astoria
Date: October 31
Phone: 325–6311
An event for all young witches and warlocks, the Monster Bash is a day-long happening with plenty of food, children's games, costume contests, and a parade that anyone dressed in Halloween garb may join. Downtown merchants decorate their shops and themselves as they dispense treats to the hundreds of trick-or-treaters invading the business district.

Astoria Regatta
Location: Waterfront, Astoria
Date: Second weekend in August
Phone: 325–6311
Where there's water, there's likely to be boat races. A tradition since 1894, the Astoria Regatta celebrates Astoria's waterfront with a week-long extravaganza of fun-filled activities certain to please every member of the family. The Regatta parade and twilight boat parade feature a small fleet of gaily-decorated craft of all types passing in review. There's a charming coronation for the Regatta Queen and her court, sailboat races, fireworks, a ship model competition, a dart tournament, tours of historic homes and buildings, and lots of food and craft booths. The youngsters will especially enjoy the excitement of the Regatta Carnival and the outrageous action at a demolition derby.

Fire Muster
Location: 30th & Marine Dr., Astoria
Date: Fourth weekend in August
Phone: 325–2203
Astoria's historic Uppertown Fire Fighters Museum (see description in this chapter) is the backdrop for the annual fire muster. The town even rolls out its venerable fire wagons for

this scorching event. Youngsters whoop it up as firefighters, decked out in their finest regalia, compete in bucket brigade races, relays, and hose cart pulling contests. It's usually warm this late in August—which is fortunate as you are likely to get wet even watching this fast-paced show.

Great Astoria Crab and Seafood Festival

Location: Warrenton City park, Second & Alder Sts.
Date: Last weekend in April
Phone: 325–6311
Cost: $3/adults, $1/ages 6–12

Considered one of the Oregon Coast's finest seafood celebrations, the Great Astoria Crab and Seafood Festival attracts nearly 20,000 visitors each year for a weekend of delicious food and merriment. From the carnival complete with children's games, clowns, and face painters to artisans and craftspeople demonstrating their talents, to dozens of food booths and a traditional crab dinner—this gala event offers something for everyone. For young flyers, a helicopter ride may well be the most memorable part of the festival.

Great Columbia Bridge Run

Location: Call for starting point
Date: Third Saturday in October
Phone: 325–6311

The Great Columbia Bridge Run, an annual interstate marathon, attracts thousands of viewers and over 1,000 participants. The course starts out from the Washington side of the Columbia River, winds through a tunnel, crosses the Astoria Bridge, and ends up at the Astoria waterfront. Although the course is 8.5 miles long, nearly half of the entrants are non-competitive walkers who cover only the bridge—a distance less than five miles. For several hours, the bridge is closed to traffic, giving trekkers spectacular views of the mighty surging Columbia without the distraction of autos whizzing by. It's a wonderful participants' event for families with older children. For those wishing to watch, the best places to be are on the

Astoria waterfront or from hillsides on the Oregon side of the course. Those wishing to be involved in this adventure must preregister at least one week in advance.

Maritime Week

Location: Columbia Maritime Museum, 1792 Marine Dr., Astoria
Date: Third week in May
Phone: 325-2323

This week-long annual festival pays homage to Astoria's two centuries of seafaring tradition. Youngsters will be thrilled to watch the United States Coast Guard conduct exciting search and rescue maneuvers. Tours of the lightship Columbia allow the junior sailors in the family to wander though the ship's bunk house, galley, and infirmary. Throughout the week there are historical films and lectures, lifesaving demonstrations, a model ship-building contest, rope-making demonstrations, a row boat competition, and plenty of live entertainment.

Scandinavian Festival

Location: Astoria High School, West Marine Dr., Astoria
Date: Third weekend in June
Phone: 325-6311

Celebrating Astoria's ethnic heritage, the Scandinavian Festival is the town's biggest, most festive event. It features craft booths and demonstrations, continuous folk dancing, a colorful parade, ethnic foods, and the crowning of Miss Scandinavia. For the children, there are lots of games and contests, clowns, and face painting. A spell-binding series of routines feature costumed dancers performing ancient rites around a high, flower-adorned pole, followed by a bonfire ceremony, and a choreographed tug of war between the various Scandinavian ethnic groups—all set to music. It's a Scandinavian shindig for families of all heritages.

2

SEASIDE

Seaside, Oregon's largest and oldest beach resort, has long attracted families to its own special blend of natural and man-made attractions. The beaches here are long and flat, attracting kite flyers, clammers, beachcombers, strollers, and three-wheeled "brike" riders. You can even drive your automobile or all terrain vehicle on certain portions of the beach . Although the ocean is always quite chilly, summer attracts hearty swimmers and surfers in droves. Lifeguards are on duty on weekends only. A short hop from the surf is Broadway Street with its wonderful collection of shops, game arcades, and eateries evocative of Atlantic City's Boardwalk. Long before the tourists came, however, Lewis and Clark visited in the winter of 1805-1806 and set up a salt cairn to extract salt from sea water. The salt was used to preserve and flavor their diet of wild game.

Sights and Attractions

Clatsop Plains Pioneer Church

Location: On Hwy 101, 7 miles north of Seaside
Days/Hours: Daily, dawn to dusk
Cost: Free

The Gray Memorial Chapel was raised on the site of the first Presbyterian Church west of the Rockies. The nearby church cemetery dating back to 1840, is the resting place for many of Seaside's early settlers. Families can share a peek into the past by strolling through this pioneer graveyard and reading the unique headstones. For families travelling along the coast, this is a nice place to stop for a rest and a bit of "buried" history.

Cleanline Surf Shop

Location: 719 1st Ave., Seaside
Phone: 738–7888
Days/Hours: Daily 10–6

There's no better way to get a wave's view of the Oregon Coast than by braving the cold ocean waters on a skim-board, boogie-board, wind-surfing board, or traditional surf board. The staff at Cleanline can provide all the particulars for those willing, able, and intrepid enough to take the plunge. All the necessary equipment, including the various boards and wetsuits can be rented here. Be prepared to take a pledge however not to divulge the secret that the north Oregon Coast offers some of the best board-riding waves in the world. The locals prefer to keep the beaches uncrowded as long as they can.

Cycling

On a cycle, be it a bicycle, tricycle, or quadricycle, you can experience a place up close. Whether you're cruising down lovely residential neighborhoods, through the various "old towns," or along the beach, you'll be treated to the unique sights and people that make up a community. A number of area rental companies offer a selection of two, three, and four wheelers for every member of the family. For a complete list of these rental firms contact the Chamber of Commerce at (800) 444–6740 or 738–6391.

Manzanita Fun Merchants
Location: 200 Ave. A and South Columbia, Seaside
Phone: 738–3703
Days/Hours: Daily 9–8 (summer), Weekends 9–6 (winter)
Rental equipment includes traditional bicycles, "jogging" strollers, and three-wheel beach fun cycles—in sizes to fit both children and adults. They even offer complimentary trailers that hook to bikes for carrying toddlers. Manzanita also has a large selection of camping gear available for rent.

Prom Bike Shop
Location: 622 12th, Seaside
Phone: 738–8251
Days/Hours: Daily 10–7
Prom Bike Shop's huge selection of rental equipment includes three-wheel cycles, trainers, tandems, all terrain bicycles, skateboards, scooters, and skates. Also available are child carriers and bicycle trailers which are enclosed, and can haul up to 150 pounds of offspring.

Seaside Surrey Rental
Location: 332 S. Columbia, Seaside
Phone: 738–0242
Days/Hours: Daily 10–7
Their rental equipment ranges from traditional 18-speed mountain bikes to 4-wheel carriages called "surreys." These quadricycles come with either two pedals or four and enable families to ride together. The four pedal model is the favorite, allowing for four pedallers and up to eight riders in a carriage. It's a novel way to cruise around town.

Estuary Park

Location: 1900 N. Holladay, Seaside
Days/Hours: Daily, dawn to dusk

Where fresh river water meets salty sea water an estuary is formed, creating a dynamic, complex ecosystem. Here at the mouth of the Necanicum River, a complete interpretive center showcases the estuary and offers explanations of its scenery and biology. From the observation deck, visitors scan salt marshes, mudflats, and look for a variety of wildlife on and around the river as it empties into the ocean. Children are delighted by the sighting of great blue and green herons, brown pelicans, and many other migratory birds. On occasion, elk, deer, otters, and beavers may also be seen from the platform. A stairway from the deck leads down to the river for a closer look at the flounder, shrimp, salmon, and plants that thrive here. The park's many interpretive signs are colorful, illustrative, and easy to comprehend. It's an educational experience for older youngsters, while the small fry enjoy romping on the walkways, bounding up and down the river stairway and catching sight of the many creatures that dwell here.

Jim's Westlake Stables

Location: Off Hwy 101, 6 miles north of Seaside
Phone: 738–6258
Days/Hours/Cost: Call for more information

Jim's Westlake Stables offers year-round rides for equestrians of all ages. For those wishing to brush up on their skills, Jim's offers individual and group riding lessons. There are no guides on these horseback rides, however, so be prepared to be your own trail boss.

Lewis and Clark Salt Works

Location: Beach Dr. and Lewis and Clark Way, Seaside
Phone: 861–2471
Days/Hours: Daily, dawn to dusk
Cost: Free

On this site in January of 1806 members of the Lewis and Clark expedition boiled sea water to obtain a priceless commodity—

salt. Back in the days before food preservation as we know it, salt was used by expedition members to improve the condition and taste of most of their foods, especially the elk, fish, and dog (*yes, dog*) they regularly ate. A replica of the original salt cairn, a cone-shaped furnace made of rocks, was reconstructed upon the site of the original. Maintained by the National Park Service, the Salt Works contains plaques describing how the expedition members were able to obtain nearly four bushels (about 20 gallons) of fine, white salt from the sea. This is a fine place for kids to learn all about a minor facet of one of the most important journeys in American history. It's hard to imagine a time without salt shakers, much less the difficulties of that winter in 1806, when a small crew labored here to replenish a vital supply of salt for the Lewis and Clark expedition.

"Million Dollar Walk"

Location: Broadway St., downtown Seaside

Though listed on the maps as "Broadway," locals call the half-mile stretch from Roosevelt Drive to the beach the "Million Dollar Walk." Be prepared for a mind-boggling collection of restaurants, fast food outlets, candy and gift shops, boutiques, and souvenir stores that await the urban hiker. The children will quickly discover Broadway's amusement centers and arcades, where they can ride bumper cars, play miniature golf, skee-ball, video games, pinballs, and engage in other games of skill. You'll have trouble getting them back out on the Broadway tour. Along your march to the sea you suddenly find yourself on the Broadway Bridge above the Necanicum River. It's a great place to feed the ducks and seagulls who have learned to prefer the ubiquitous caramel corn, peanut brittle, and cotton candy to the healthier morsels we suggest you proffer. At the westernmost end of Broadway is the famous Turnaround (also known as "Times Square of Oregon"), a small traffic circle ringed with well-populated benches that are ideal for people watching and soaking up the sun, or watching it slip beneath the waves. This spot also marks the official end of the celebrated Lewis and Clark Trail.

Monkey Business Rentals

Location: Quat at Marine Park, between First & Ave. A, Seaside
Phone: 738–8209
Days/Hours: Daily 12–8 (summer only)

Every summer this boat rental company readies a small fleet of bumper boats to do battle on the Necanicum River. The one-person boat is powered by a two-horsepower motor giving just enough oomph for a splashy, satisfying head-on collision with another ship. Both the bumper and bumpee are usually drenched upon impact—which is why it's a good idea to wear T-shirts and shorts while in combat. Small children can climb aboard "buddy boats" which are designed to hold an adult and a child. Monkey Business also rents kayaks, paddle boats, and rowboats for those wishing to just peacefully explore the river. Whatever type of vessel you choose, you and your family can have a wonderful time on the Necanicum.

The Promenade

Location: Along the beach, Seaside

Seaside's most notable man-made attraction is a scenic concrete boardwalk that borders the beach for a mile and a half. For decades, walking the "Prom" has been a must on every sightseer's agenda. On one side are spectacular views of sand, surf, and coastal headlands, while fine old hotels and residences line the other. Of late, modern resorts with their glittering glass and steel have located alongside these genteel originals. A facelift in 1985 brought a new, clean look to the Prom, including new benches, rest areas, and restrooms. For young visitors however, this walkway is much better suited as a runway. Bikers and skaters love to race from one end to the other, dodging the ever-present slower-moving obstacles along the way. If you want to join the wheeled traffic, see "cycling" earlier in this chapter.

Seagull Harbor

Location: On Hwy 101, 3 miles south of Seaside
Phone: 738–7663
Days/Hours: Daily 10–6, 10–9 (summer)

Seagull Harbor can't be missed. It's the eye-catching place along Highway 101 adorned with richly-painted lawn ornaments and brightly-colored flags fluttering in the wind. On these premises stands a gull factory where whimsical ornamental seagulls are created. There's also a large gift shop stocked with basic souvenirs as well as nautical chimes, ship wheels, porthole clocks, and glass fishing floats. But the real excitement is around back at the World of Fun where a collection of fast, action-packed rides are guaranteed to attract youngsters of all ages. A perennial favorite is "Krazy Kars"— circular, gas powered carts that skim along the slick driving surface ramming into other cars. Other attractions include 5-horsepower racing go-carts (that really move!) and a 19-hole miniature golf course. Also, there are several kiddie rides to entertain the small children.

Seaside Aquarium

Location: 200 N. Promenade, Seaside
Phone: 738–6211
Days/Hours: Sun–Thurs 9–6, Fri & Sat 9–8 (summer); Wed–Sun 9–5 (rest of year)
Cost: $4.50/adults, $2.25/ages 6–11
Built in 1937, the Seaside Aquarium is home to an excellent representation of Northwest marine life, including moray eels, wolf fish, rare sea turtles, leopard sharks, and an octopus. These denizens of the deep are housed in huge glass-fronted reservoirs through which nearly 75,000 gallons of ocean water are pumped each day. Of special interest to children is a roomful of barking, wheezing harbor seals who carry on amusing song-and-dance routines to get the kids to toss them the small fish morsels sold at the Aquarium. Another popular attraction here is a large touch tank where youngsters may reach in and shake hands with some pretty exotic sea creatures.

Seaside Historical Museum

Location: Necanicum Dr. & Fifth St., Seaside
Phone: 738–7065
Days/Hours: Daily 10:30–4:30
Cost: $1/adults, 50¢/ages 16 & under

Through old photographs, antiques, and other historical items, visitors can travel back in time to witness Seaside's development from its prehistoric days as an Indian settlement to its present status as the quintessential beach resort. This museum has lots of kid-appeal displays. Centuries old Indian artifacts (excavated by archaeologists who came from the Smithsonian Institute) are themselves worth the price of admission. The exhibit of fire fighting equipment that dates back nearly a century stands in stark contrast with the modern technology now available to firefighters. Old photographs of Seaside and its people are silent reminders of a quieter, simpler age long past. A fully-equipped "antique" print shop will have computer-age children wondering how long it took to produce newspapers and books in those days. Adjacent to the museum is the Butterfield Cottage, a complete restoration of one of the original beach cottages of Seaside. The cottage is such an exact reproduction of the house it once was that upon entering you'll feel like you were back in the early years of this century. Both museum and cottage are delightful stops, and particularly educational for the older children.

Seaside Town Center

Location: 300 Broadway, Seaside
Phone: 738–6278

Set along Broadway's "Million Dollar Walk" (see description in this chapter) this enclosed mall houses 20 unique stores, restaurants, and specialty shops. There are merchants who market kites, wind socks, toys, balloons, and games, as well as a tempting array of shops offering cookies, ice cream, and yogurt. However, it's the picturesque carousel that grabs the attention and the imagination of riders of all ages. The lively horses, frolicking animals, sparkling lights, mirrors, and music—all promenading beneath a giant skylight—are irresistible.

Track and Trail Stables

Location: Off Hwy 101, 3 miles south of Seaside
Phone: 738–6336
Days/Hours/Cost: Call for more information
Seaside's picturesque surroundings seem even more appealing from atop a cantering steed. Track and Trail offers family beach rides and trail rides through verdant coastal forest. Young or inexperienced riders not quite ready to hit the sand or trails can enjoy an optional ride around the track.

Parks and Camping

Cartwright Park

Location: South Franklin near Avenue U, Seaside
This south side park is a favorite for rafters, canoers, and other river lovers. It also offers a boat ramp down to the Necanicum River. For the youngsters, a nice playground area and a large playing field provide opportunities to burn off some energy. A picnic shelter and restrooms round out the amenities at this fine neighborhood park.

Broadway Park

Location: 1140 Broadway, Seaside
Situated on the banks of the Neawanna Creek, Broadway Park is a favorite spot for a picnic and a day of fun for the entire family. There are covered picnic sites, restrooms, basketball hoops, volleyball courts, ball fields, tennis courts, and a horseshoe pit with horseshoes. Two separate areas with playground equipment will appeal to both big and little kids. If you grow tired of all this playing, a multi-station exercise unit for adults and children may be just the tonic. Be sure to bring bread scraps or other morsels for the ducks. A large contingent of these waterfowl is usually on hand at the creek waiting patiently for a free meal. You'll be completely surrounded by quacking, ravenous ducks.

Goodman Park

Location: 12th Ave. & Necanicum Dr., Seaside

This fine park on Seaside's north end is a lovely place for a picnic or just kicking back on a grassy knoll with your toes dipped in the Necanicum River. Goodman Park has picnic areas, a playing field, restrooms, basketball hoops, lots of benches, and a playground. It's usually uncrowded here except for a few fishermen atop the 12th Avenue Bridge fishing the Necanicum, making it a quiet place for a bite and a rest if you're travelling.

Saddle Mountain State Park

Location: North of Hwy 26, 12 miles east of Seaside
Cost: Free/day use, $9/camping

This state park is renowned for its spectacular, exhilarating hike to the top of Saddle Mountain, the highest peak in Oregon's Coast Range. The wind-whipped panoramic view from atop this 3,283 perch is truly awe-inspiring. But you'll have to work for it. The hike up is along a trail in primitive condition. The arduous 2.5 mile ascent, in places very steep and narrow, is not recommended for small children, though teenagers and older hikers in good condition will find the ascent challenging and exciting. Along the way, hikers will be treated to dense forest, grassy meadows brimming with wildflowers in season, and the sight of huge, rocky crags—the likes of which will make you think you're on the Matterhorn. Don't be surprised to cross paths with any number of creatures living on Saddle Mountain, including deer, elk, or coyotes. At the base of the mountain are restrooms, picnic sites, and ten primitive tent campsites. To get there, take Highway 26 to the highway sign just past milepost 15. From there, it's about a seven mile drive to the base of Saddle Mountain.

Quatat Marine Park

Location: Between First & A Avenues, Seaside

Situated on the banks of the Necanicum River, Quatat marine Park has restrooms, picnic sites, seating areas, a large deck, and a floating boat dock. Wooden walkways along the river span three bridges, offering the youngsters a great place to let off some steam. In summer, everyone can enjoy exploring the river aboard paddle boats available dockside from Monkey Business Rentals (see description in this chapter). Also, free Saturday concerts at 2 p.m. from July to September are held on the park's stage. A variety of musicians and entertainers will delight the whole family against a backdrop of the Necanicum peacefully meandering by.

Annual Events

Gingerbread Christmas
Location: Butterfield Cottage, 570 Necanicum, Seaside
Date: December weekends thru Christmas
Phone: (800) 444–6740 or 738–7065
Decorated as an old-fashioned gingerbread house, this restored, historic cottage becomes the magical setting each Christmas season for Seaside's gingerbread festival. Volunteers from the town's Historical Society dress in styles from another century and serve gingerbread treats and hot drinks. It's a charming event for children who'll enjoy the many fanciful entries in a gingerbread house competition.

Lewis and Clark Historical Pageant
Location: Broadway Park, 1140 Broadway, Seaside
Date: July thru August
Phone: (800) 444–6740 or 738–5869
Cost: $7.50/adults, $3/ages 6–16
Seaside's major event of the year re-enacts the exciting and hazardous journey of Lewis and Clark, the famous explorers sent west in 1805 by President Thomas Jefferson. This engaging historical drama takes place outdoors along the banks of the scenic Neawanna Creek. Children will enjoy the colorful, authentic costuming, scenery, and the occasional comic scenes and dialogue. Attending one of these performances is an excellent way for youngsters to learn about history in an

entertaining manner. Showtime is at 8 p.m. on Thursday, Friday, and Saturday evenings, with 2 p.m. matinees on Sunday and Monday.

Seaside's Christmas Gift Fair

Location: Seaside Convention Center
Date: Weekend after Thanksgiving
Phone: (800) 444–6740 or 738–6391
The Convention Center is the site of over 100 craftspeople selling and demonstrating a huge array of hand crafted items—just in time for Christmas shopping. This seasonal event has something for every member of the family. Santa will drop by to visit with the youngsters, while strolling carolers spread holiday cheer to every nook and cranny in this building. Young shoppers eye the many unique, whimsical articles on display—especially the toys. In addition, fair goers will find food booths, plenty of live music, and a roomful of children's games guaranteed to entertain the youngsters for hours.

Seaside Fourth of July

Location: Turnaround Beach, west end of Broadway, Seaside
Date: July 4th
Phone: (800) 444–6740 or 738–6391
Seasiders pull out all the stops for this gala Independence Day celebration. After a full day of contests, games, crafts, and foods galore, the real show begins. The town's fireworks have gained notoriety throughout the state, so thousands gather on this wide beach to marvel at the pyrotechnic display. As the rockets burst overhead, their brilliant, dazzling colors reflect on the ocean—and choruses of oohs and aahs ripple from the crowd. It's a terrific, blazing show for the whole family—so hot, in fact, that the Seaside Fire Department is in charge of running this sound and light spectacle.

3

CANNON BEACH

In spite of its impressive growth that began over a decade ago, Cannon Beach remains a quaint little community of whitewashed-wood cottages and shops surrounded by picturesque landscapes. Due to the inspirational appeal of its natural beauty, Cannon Beach has become home to a large colony of well-known artists, writers, and musicians who've transformed the town into a major cultural destination for the Northwest. Offshore, another resident has become famous as one of the world's largest monoliths—Haystack Rock. While some are content to see Cannon Beach as just perfect for quiet strolls amidst natural grandeur, others see it as a gold mine of recreational opportunities. Visitors to the seven-mile beach can enjoy jogging, horseback riding, hiking, beachcombing, kite flying, picnicking, evening bonfires, and a variety of seasonal events and festivals. The resort town is named for a small cannon which washed ashore south of the community following the shipwreck of a U.S. Navy sloop-of-war in 1846.

Sights and Attractions

The Coaster Theater
Location: 108 N. Hemlock, Cannon Beach
Phone: 436–1242
Cost: Admission prices vary; call for information
One of the jewels in Cannon Beach's cultural crown is the Coaster Theater, one of the finest community theaters in the Pacific Northwest. It's a rustic, charming theater that seats a mere 200—giving the performers and audience close rapport. The Coaster endeavors to offer year-round entertainment suitable for the whole family. Among its annual stock of plays, concerts, dance and comedy performances and musical revues, are several productions that will please young theatergoers. During the holiday season, the Coaster plays a special role in the town's Victorian Christmas celebration. Following a gala lamplighting ceremony and Dickens' Soiree, celebrants march over to the Coaster for a special adaptation of Dickens' "A Christmas Carol." This is first-rate family entertainment that brings back devotees year after year.

Cycling
See introduction to "Cycling" in Chapter 2.

Manzanita Fun Merchants
Location: 1140 S. Hemlock, Cannon Beach
Phone: 436–1880
Days/Hours: Daily 9-8 (summer), Weekends 9-6 (winter)
Manzanita's rental equipment includes traditional bikes, "jogging" strollers, and beach fun tricycles for children and adults. They offer complimentary trailers that hook to bikes for carrying toddlers. Camping gear is also available.

Mike's Bike Shop
Location: 248 N. Spruce, Cannon Beach
Phone: 436–1266
Days/Hours: Daily 10-6

A full-service bike shop offering three-wheel beach bikes, mountain bikes, and single speed beach cruisers for rent. At no additional charge you can obtain trailers with room for two youngsters. Phone ahead for reservations.

The Haystack Program

Location: Various Cannon Beach locations
Phone: 725–4081, (800) 452–4909, or (800) 547–8887 (outside Oregon)
Days/Hours/Cost: Call for specifics (July thru August)

For nearly a quarter-century, Portland State University's Haystack Program has offered residents and visitors alike enriching courses in music, art, writing, theater arts, and environmental studies. Classes are taught in small group settings and run anywhere from one day to two weeks, providing adults the opportunity to explore or develop new talents and skills. Such perennial favorites as mystery writing, choral conducting, fiction techniques, poetry writing, and classes in fiddle, steel drum, guitar, and banjo draw participants from diverse lifestyles, experience levels, and age groups. While Mom and Dad are learning, sharing, and growing in their studies, youngsters age three to twelve may pursue special activities on their own. The program offers films, field trips, arts and crafts, nature walks, and beachcombing. It's an educational, absolutely hands-on experience.

Haystack Rock

Location: Just offshore, .5 miles south of Cannon Beach

One of the world's largest coastal monoliths rises 235 feet out of the sea as it looms offshore just south of town. Protected as a wildlife refuge, Haystack Rock is home to several bird species that nest there during the summer. Its tidepools teem with a rich diversity of intertidal creatures including starfish, crabs, chitons, limpets, and exotic invertebrate animals. It's a fascinating spot for kids and grown-ups, too. But, for those of you who aren't quite sure what chitons or limpets are, the Haystack Rock Interpretive Programs may be just the thing. On most summer weekends, especially low tide mornings, program staff members assemble at the rock's tidepools to point out intertidal life forms, collect specimens for a portable aquarium, and answer such questions as: "what's that," and "who lives where and why," and "what do they eat" (or "who eats whom,") and a million others like them. These interesting programs are not only great fun, they're also educational.

Neahkahnie Mountain
Location: Off Hwy 101, 8 miles south of Cannon Beach
Often cloud-capped, Neahkahnie Mountain is identified in Indian legends as the "Home of the Gods." Early settlers along this portion of the coast were intrigued with, and frightened by, this place. The headland has been a place of mystery and fascination for other reasons as well. Local stories, some with historical support, capture the imagination of young explorers. One of the most popular legends insists that survivors of an early 18th century shipwrecked Spanish galleon buried their treasure chest somewhere at the base of Neahkahnie Mountain. While many adventurers have searched, none have found the fabled riches. A short (about two miles) but challenging trail winds through a coastal rain forest en route to the mountaintop perch 1,800 feet above the sea. Along the way the switch-backing trail reveals views of meadows that explode with colorful wildflowers in season, elk browsing on the slopes, and ships sailing off the seacoast. It's a magical trek ideally suited for older children. To reach the trailhead, look for a small highway sign just north of Oswald West viewpoint on Highway 101 (four miles north of Manzanita).

Sea Ranch Stables
Location: Along Ecola Creek, north end of Cannon Beach
Phone: 436–1268
Days/Hours: Daily 9–5 (May thru September)
Cost: Call for prices
Riders of all skill levels are welcome to take part in Sea Ranch's guided horseback rides through dense coastal forest or along the beach. With horses available for all ages, Sea Ranch can match the right horse for each rider. The trails lead through

spectacular coastal scenery. It's an ideal way for families to spend leisure time together and see Oregon's beauty from a different perspective. Prices vary depending on length of ride and route taken. While reservations aren't required, it's best to call ahead regarding availability.

Parks and Camping

Arcadia Beach State Park
Location: Off Hwy 101, 1 mile south of Cannon Beach
The 19 acres that make up tiny Arcadia Beach State Park sit atop a squat bluff above the sand. A short trail leads to an uncrowded beach notable for its unusual rock formations, teeming tidepools, and productive beachcombing. It's a great place for children to explore with Mom and Dad, or picnic, stroll, or just plain relax on the beach. Restrooms and water are available.

Cannon Beach City Park
Location: Second and Spruce Sts., Cannon Beach
City Park has something for everyone: tennis courts, a ball field, basketball courts, restrooms, and a drinking fountain. There's also a nice picnic area with play equipment that both big and little children will enjoy. And if among your trunkful of tennis rackets, tennis balls, baseballs, bats, gloves, and basketballs you remember to bring the kids' skateboards—you're in luck. The skateboard park in City Park is awesome.

Ecola State Park
Location: Off Hwy 101, 2 miles north of Cannon Beach
Phone: 436–2623
This 1,300 acre park covers much of Tillamook Head, a massive point of land that reaches out into the Pacific. Perched on this promontory, Ecola Park has one of the most expansive and magnificent coastal views imaginable. With restrooms, fountains, and picnic areas, as well as acres of trees, grass, and trails, Ecola Park is an ideal site for a picnic and a day of fun.

Bring along binoculars to get a closer look at the sea lion and bird rookeries located on the off-shore rocks. Everyone loves the sight of sea lions basking on surf-drenched rocks. From this point you've also got a front-row seat for catching sight of migrating gray whales. And don't be surprised if you come face to face with some four-legged land rovers. The park is frequented by deer who roam it at will. For those traveling with older children who love a good hike (this one's several hours each way), a beautiful trail winds its way through the park and connects with the Tillamook Head Trail over the cape. The trail leads to secluded beaches and coves before climbing over the Head. This was the same route that explorers Lewis and Clark took when they came here in 1806.

Hug Point State Park

Location: Off Hwy 101, 4 miles south of Cannon Beach

Hug Point wasn't named for romantic reasons. A likely explanation is that visitors have to stay very close to one another when hiking the short, steep trail to the beach. The cliffs here are gouged with tidal caves that young explorers love to examine. This is safe *only* at low tide, as these grottos are cut off when the tide returns. In addition, Hug Point State Park possesses a waterfall, an old, rough-hewn roadbed over the cliff face, as well as such creature comforts as drinking water, picnic sites, and restrooms. Although there are only 42 acres here, this diminutive hillside park offers big adventures.

Klootchy Creek Park

Location: On Hwy 26, 2 miles east of Cannon Beach

Many coastal travellers come to this 25 acre forest to take a look at two of the world's largest Sitka spruce trees. These verdant skyscrapers rise over 220 feet and measure 50 feet around at the base. It's an awe-inspiring sight. Perhaps as mind-boggling is the fact that these trees are over 700 years old—remnants of an enormous forest that once covered the land long before Christopher Columbus ever arrived in the New World. The whole family will enjoy traversing the short (about 800 feet long) nature trail that starts at the southeast corner of the main parking area. A narrative trail guide available at the trail head describes the different native plants and natural forest processes occurring in the park. The upper Necanicum River flows through the park, offering swimming and steelhead and salmon fishing. With picnic sites aplenty, Klootchy Creek Park is truly a lovely place for an outing.

Les Shirley Park

Location: 5th St. and Ecola Creek, Cannon Beach

A marker at Les Shirley park commemorates the site where Lewis and Clark first purchased from the Indians an exotic seafood—whale blubber. This park has picnic tables and barbecue grills, restrooms, and open, grassy areas that make ideal running areas for small legs. From Les Shirley Park it's just a short walk to the beach or to downtown. An even easier way to get to town is to hop aboard the free shuttle that starts here at the park. Look for the white vans with blue and green lettering. They run every half hour in the summer and less often the rest of the year.

Nehalem Bay State Park

Location: 2 miles off Hwy 101 at Bayshore Junction, Nehalem Bay
Phone: 368–5943
Cost: Free/day use, $13/camping (April thru November)

Located on a four-mile long sand spit that separates Nehalem Bay from the sea, this state park features over 300 full-hookup campsites with picnic tables, fireplaces, and water. Day users will find several picnic areas, restrooms, water, and large parking lots. For those travelling with the family horse in tow, Nehalem Bay State Park also has a horse camp, with corrals and miles of bridle paths.

Recreational opportunities abound here. Nehalem Bay provides excellent crabbing and clamming. Park staff can show where and how to capture and cook these elusive marine delicacies. The kids will enjoy hiking and exploring a large sand dune that lies between the campground and the ocean. Once over the dune, real treasures await young beachcombers. Glass Japanese fishing floats, agates and driftwood are commonly found here. And with a bit of luck, a youngster might come upon a chunk of beeswax from a sunken 16th century Spanish merchant ship.

Oswald West State Park

Location: Off Hwy 101, 10 miles south of Cannon Beach
Phone: 368–5153
Cost: Free/day use, $9/camping (March thru October)
Within Oswald West State Park's 2,500 mostly undeveloped acres are 36 primitive campsites with restrooms, picnic sites, and water. Several trails wind through marvelous old growth woods, so primeval that it gets a little eerie at times, but offers adventure for young hikers. Another trail, no more than just a short walk in reality, leads to Smuggler's Cove where a wide shallow creek provides a wading place for small children. This beautiful, secluded cove is a great place for grown-ups to picnic or just kick back and enjoy the spectacular rain forest scenery while the youngsters splash and search for rocks in the creek. The trail continues for two miles to rugged Cape Falcon, a well known navigational landmark that's home to a dense, ancient forest of giant sitka spruce. Many of these trees are over 12 feet around at the base and 200 feet tall.

Tolovana State Park

Location: Off Hwy 101, 2 miles south of Cannon Beach
This postage stamp sized park offers restrooms, water, a grassy area, and lovely picnic sites bordering on the beach. Thanks to its easy beach access, impatient youngsters can reach the surf in a jiffy. Tolovana State Park is also an excellent starting point for a delightful three mile beach walk to Hug Point (see description in this chapter). Along the way the kids will be delighted with the productive beachcombing and profusion of tidepools teeming with tiny marine life. Heading out in the opposite direction will bring you closer and closer to the huge offshore monolith, Haystack Rock (see description in this chapter).

Whale Park

Location: N. Hemlock and Third, Cannon Beach
The park is well-known for its arresting sculpture of a whale that commemorates the spot where explorers Lewis and Clark sighted an immense beached whale in 1806. Whale Park is also a favorite rendezvous for the locals who like to sink into the cozy seating areas to watch gorgeous, panoramic Cannon Beach sunsets. There's also a beach access here that wastes no time getting the kids onto the sand. Several local outfits (see "cycling" in this chapter) rent three-wheel beach bikes and beach cruisers that enable youngsters to zip along the beach like a bullet train to Tokyo. Complimentary trailers (with room for two children) that hook on to bikes are also available.

Annual Events

Nehalem Arts Festival

Location: Various locations in Nehalem
Date: Second weekend in July
Phone: 368–5100
The population of this tiny town increases by fifty-fold the weekend of this popular annual arts fest. Over 100 artisans and craftspeople display their wares of art, pottery, fabric, and wood along sidewalks from one end of crowded Nehalem to the other. Especially interesting for the children are the many craft demonstrations that fill the sidewalks and parking lots. They'll be treated to spinners threading wool through spinning wheels, potters shaping and throwing gobs of wet clay, painters wielding paint brushes, and woodworkers whittling away at chunks of wood. Strolling musicians, frisky clowns, balloons everywhere, and appetizing aromas add to the merriment at this citywide block party.

Puffin Kite Festival

Location: On the beach (off Hemlock St.), Cannon Beach
Date: Last weekend in April
Phone: 436–2623

One of the most fun-filled annual kite festivals in the Northwest opens with a nighttime kite fly, embellished by a blazing bonfire and a child-pleasing marshmallow roast on the beach. The festivities resume the next morning with a pancake breakfast, and continue throughout the day with kite flying demonstrations and competitions. Though not quite a pitched battle, the rivalry can get fierce as contestants compete for prizes in a variety of events, including highest flying kite, quickest reeling in, kite relay races, and the night flight kite contest. A break in the action allows young spectators to get involved in some activities of their own: an ice cream social, a kids' "color a kite" contest, and an outdoor barbecue. The final day's events feature a number of judged events, such as best homemade kite, most amusing, ugliest, and most unusual. The youngest and oldest kite flyers also receive prizes. The festival finale features a delightful kite treasure hunt—an enjoyable challenge for young and old alike.

Sandcastle Day

Location: On the beach, a mile north of Haystack Rock, Cannon Beach
Date: A Saturday in late May
Phone: 436–2623

Known the world over, the Cannon Beach Sandcastle Day attracts over 1,000 participants who create some of the finest sand sculptures imaginable. Over 20,000 spectators would heartily agree. Youngsters watch in fascination as such perennial favorites as Cinderella and her carriage, Darth Vader, Humpty Dumpty, and other magical creatures are fashioned right before their eyes. And for those young castle builders wishing to join the action, registration is open practically right up to the day of the event. Younger kids are included in the Junior Division and compete against children their own age. The rules are simple: build whatever you want on your plot of sand using only water and simple hand tools, forms, and buckets; for decoration, use only items natural to the beach, such as driftwood, shells, agates, or seaweed. Entrants have four hours to complete their works, followed by judging and awarding of prizes. It's a creative, fun day that will long live in the memories of these young builders. Memories will have to do, since by early afternoon the incoming tides will have obliterated each and every masterpiece. Sandcastle Day events are free to spectators, but contestants pay a small fee.

Summer Concerts In The Park
Location: City Park, downtown Cannon Beach
Date: Sundays 2–4 pm (July thru Labor Day)
Phone: 436–2623
As soon as the music begins wafting through the downtown area, locals and visitors alike load the picnic basket and head for the blue and white bandshell in City Park. Youngsters will enjoy munching while listening to classical, pops, or children's concert pieces. Especially for travel-weary grown-ups, these outdoor park concerts make restful family breaks for an hour or two.

4

TILLAMOOK

Within the greater Tillamook area lie 70 miles of scenic coastline, seven rivers, and four bays. It's no wonder the early Indians gave it the name Tillamook, meaning "Land of Many Waters." Besides water, Tillamook has cows, lots of them; more cows than residents, in fact. In addition to being the center of Oregon's dairy industry, Tillamook is a major recreation center offering fishing, boating, clamming, beachcombing, hiking, hang gliding, windsurfing, canoeing, and of course, cheese sampling. After each of the devastating forest fires east of town in 1933 (the fire raged out of control for four weeks), 1939, and 1945, undaunted residents planted seedlings in an attempt to bring life back to the ravaged areas. Today, impressive stands of trees endure as a living testimonial to the community's visionary reforestation efforts.

Sights and Attractions

Blimp Hangars

Location: Tillamook Bay Industrial Park, off Hwy 101; 2 miles
south of Tillamook

Two enormous buildings can be seen several miles south of
town from Highway 101. These monsters, squatting in the
distance, were built during the second World War to house the
United States Navy blimps used along the coast to watch for
Japanese submarines. Considered the largest free-standing
wooden structures in the world, they now shelter some interesting business ventures. Luxury railroad cars are refurbished
in one; the other houses commercial blimps used in advertising, logging, surveillance, and rescue work.

The hangars are located in an industrial park that still
maintains the original buildings, utilities, and streets that date
from the days the area was a Naval Air Station. Although the
blimp hangars are not officially open to public tours, the
hangar doors are kept open for ventilation. A quick peek will
leave you open-mouthed at the size of these cavernous super-
structures. There's enough space to hold a 20 story office
building and seven football fields side by side. And who knows,
you may even get to see a blimp flying out on assignment.

Blue Heron French Cheese Company

Location: Off Hwy 101, 1 mile north of Tillamook
Days/Hours: Daily 8–8 (summer), 9–6 (winter)
Phone: 842–8281

Welcome to a free taste of Oregon. Some of the state's finest
specialty foods, including Brie and Camembert cheeses, mus-
tards, honeys, jams, spice mixes, and fruit products, await the
serious sampler in Blue Heron's tasting room. In another
room, grown-ups may partake of a selection of wine samples
from Oregon's leading vineyards. The company is housed in
an old Dutch barn, now painted white with large Blue Heron
logos on each of the gable ends, making it easy for those with
rumbling stomachs to locate.

Cape Kiwanda

Location: Three Cape Loop, 15 miles southwest of Tillamook
Spectacular views, steep sand dunes, and a quiet beach are a few of the reasons for Cape Kiwanda's immense popularity. The headland juts out into the sea protecting the beach to its south from the full wrath of wind and waves. Offshore lies another Haystack Rock, like its namesake to the north, that further defends the beach from punishing waves. As a result, the surf south of Cape Kiwanda is incredibly docile, making it a splashing playground for the kids. Come early in the morning and you'll witness fishermen launching their flat-bottomed boats, called "dories," into the open surf directly from the beach. There are only a few other places on the planet where this can be done. The most interesting part is the return late in the afternoon. Crowds gather to watch the returning dories sailing at full-throttle towards the beach, then skidding along the sand like a landing seaplane on ice. When done according to plan, the arrival is spectacular, even artistic. But, when fish-laden vessels come ashore poorly, it can be quite a mess. The kids will love the excitement. Cape Kiwanda is also the jumping-off place for hang glider enthusiasts. If just relaxing and watching the hang gliders soar by from off the cape isn't enough action, there are shops in nearby Oceanside and Pacific City that can provide all the gear and lessons for older daredevils to get up there and try it themselves.

Latimer Quilt and Textile Center

Location: Wilson River Loop Rd., Tillamook
Phone: 842–7525
Days/Hours: Call for hours
Cost: Free
Occupying the historic Maple Leaf School, the Latimer Center houses a research library, an unusually rich collection of quilts and fabrics, quilt blocks, and many other associated materials. The fabrics are arranged by decades, beginning from 1850 and include a remarkable selection of pioneer quilts. Of special interest to the kids are the center's hands-on demonstrations of quilting, spinning, weaving, rug making, basketry, and

needlework. The staff seems to go all out to make these demonstrations educational and fun for youngsters.

Memorial Lumberman's Park

Location: Third and American Sts., Garibaldi
Phone: 322–0301
Days/Hours: Daily, dawn to dusk

This terrific museum houses a fine collection of old logging and railroading equipment in an attractive park setting. Youngsters will love racing through the railway coach and wooden caboose as well as climbing all over a steam engine and steam logging donkey. A picnic area offers a quiet spot for grown-ups to relax while the kids are releasing energy.

Munson Creek Falls

Location: Munson Creek Rd., 6.5 miles south of Tillamook

Munson Creek Falls, one of Oregon's highest waterfalls, drops 266 feet over spectacularly rugged, verdant cliffs. A sign on the east side of Highway 101 directs motorists to Munson Creek Road leading to the falls—about 1.5 miles away. Take the trail from the middle of the parking area for a short stroll through a lush, green gorge to the base of the falls. It's an easy one-half mile walk that even small legs can handle. A well-maintained picnic area makes a perfect base camp for grown-ups and ice chests while the youngsters explore nearby. While the falls are a delight to behold in any season, come visit in winter when heavy runoffs shoot down like an express train, and freezing temperatures transform the mist-shrouded cliffs and trees into a crystal ice palace.

Octopus Tree

Location: Cape Meares State Park, 9 miles northwest of Tillamook

Certainly one of the more memorable natural sights in Oregon, the legendary Octopus Tree has been mystifying visitors for centuries. This giant, cliff-top Sitka Spruce, battered by coastal weather, grew like a bizarre candelabrum. It has no central trunk, but instead has five-foot thick limbs that branch out close to the ground before turning skyward. Youngsters like to believe the Indian legends that say the octopus is a burial tree, shaped, in its youth to hold the canoes of dead Indian chiefs. In reality, no one is certain of the eerie giant's age; some suggest it was a young tree at about the time of Christ. A visit to the Octopus Tree can be an enchanting, magical stop.

Oregon Coastline Express
Location: Southern Pacific Depot, E. 3rd St. in Tillamook
Phone: 842–2768
Days/Hours/Cost: Daily departures, call for fares and times
This little 44-mile round trip railroad line offers riders a scenic coastline run between Tillamook and Wheeler. The picturesque route passes dairy farms, quaint bayfront communities, and the Pacific Ocean shore. With stops along the way in Garibaldi and Rockaway, the journey is great fun for the kids, Mom and Dad, and all dedicated railroad buffs. In addition, a shorter excursion known as the "Caboose Run" covers a three mile stretch of track—in rebuilt cabooses—past sawmills, dairy pasture, and to the blimp hangars (see description in this chapter) for a tour of these amazing structures. The caboose train's extra-large picture windows will insure you don't miss a thing. It's an interesting little trip packed with rewarding sights.

Pioneer Museum
Location: 2106 Second St., Tillamook
Phone: 842–4553
Days/Hours: Mon–Sat 8:30–5, Sun 12–5
Cost: $1/adults, 50¢/ages 12–17
This splendid three-story white stone building was once the county courthouse. Today, it is home to one of the finest museums in Oregon and contains a wealth of exhibits that will strike the fancy of every member of the family. On the upper level a natural history collection includes wildlife and bird displays (and some pretty ferocious-looking mounted grizzly

bears) as well as fossils, and animal skulls. The rock and mineral collection will attract young rockhounds. On the main floor are relics once belonging to an Indian Chief, as well as early pioneer artifacts like shoes, dolls, musical instruments, and children's toys. There's a pioneer home, workshop, and barn that youngsters love to explore. The antique gun collection provides a fascinating look at early weaponry, while the military collection displays more modern items, including military gear and a Scud fragment from the Desert Storm operation in the Persian Gulf. Downstairs, early automobiles, a stage coach, a blacksmith shop, and an authentic, full-size fire lookout station have plenty of kid-appeal.

Alongside the museum, a steam donkey awaits inspection. Once used in the logging industry to pull logs across mountainsides or over canyons, the donkey gave way to more efficient diesel-powered machinery. But as in the days of yore, you'll be able to watch it being fired up. It's an impressive sight to behold the reciprocating engines, the steam puffing out, and the whistles screaming. Young visitors can even blow the whistles themselves.

Three Arch Rocks Wildlife Refuge

Location: Ocean State Park, Ocean Loop Rd. in Oceanside
These rocks (actually more like mini-islands) sprawl one-half mile offshore at Oceanside (8 miles west of Tillamook) and are home to many species of birds and other wildlife. As viewed through binoculars from the sandy beaches of Ocean State Park, the refuge can be seen teeming with hundreds of thousands of nesting seabirds as well as herds of sea lions and seals basking along the sun-drenched rocks. It's a captivating view of marine wildlife. In addition, much of the year sea lion pups can be seen frolicking in the surf along the beach. But that's not the end to this adventure. Take a short hike to the north end of this small beach where a tunnel through the cliff leads to another beach. It's a passageway the kids will love to explore.

Three Capes Loop

Location: Byway off Hwy 101, between Neskowin and Tillamook

A trip to Tillamook is just not complete without a tour of the Three Capes Loop—considered by many to be the foremost scenic area on Oregon's north coast. It's a pleasant drive with lots to see and do. This 36 mile ocean frontage road connects Capes Kiwanda, Lookout, and Meares as it meanders through dairy country, dense forestland, and small beach communities. Of course the chief attractions here are the three capes themselves—which should be experienced outside the car on foot in order to appreciate the uniqueness of each. Cape Kiwanda's wave-battered sandstone cliffs, Lookout's rocky headland piercing the sea for two miles, and Meares' freakish, monstrous Silka spruce are but pieces in an immense coastal puzzle accessible to young and old alike.

Tillamook Cheese Factory

Location: On Hwy 101, 2 miles north of Tillamook
Phone: 842–4481
Days/Hours: Daily 8–8 (summer), 8–6 (rest of year)

What do most Northwesterners think of when they hear "Tillamook?" Cheese, of course. And to let folks in on how the delectable stuff is actually made, this large cheese maker welcomes visitors to watch the whole process—from milk curds and whey, to pressing, cheddaring, and splitting into huge blocks of cheese. Youngsters will enjoy the view from the glass enclosed observation platform looking down on a bee-hive of white-uniformed cheesemakers scurrying about the cavernous factory. A short video details all the goings-on below. Also, an interesting self-guided tour details the history of the factory and cheesemaking in Tillamook County. You will see historic cheese production equipment as well as a facsimile dairy cow being milked. Besides cheese, there's butter, ice cream, and a multitude of yummy cheese spreads all made here and available fresh at the ice cream counter, deli, and gift shop. Outside the factory is a seaworthy replica of the Morning Star, a wooden ship built by early butter and cheesemakers to ship their products to distant ports.

Whiskey Creek Fish Hatchery

Location: Whiskey Creek Rd., Tillamook
Phone: 824–4033
Days/Hours: Daily 8–5
Cost: Free

Whether or not your children have ever been to a fish hatchery, they'll enjoy a visit to this one. Operated by Oregon State University, the hatchery rears over 100,000 spring Chinook each year for release in Tillamook Bay streams. From viewing areas around the rearing ponds, youngsters can watch how the baby fish are fed and cared for until they're released in late August. In addition, there's a park with picnic sites, many fine educational displays, and several spots along Whiskey Creek where visitors can see chum salmon returning in the autumn. It's a fascinating stop.

Cape Lookout State Park

Location: Whiskey Creek Rd., south of Tillamook
Phone: 842–3182
Cost: Free/day use, $9–13/camping

Cape Lookout is one of the most popular and remote coastal parks in Oregon. The Cape contains examples of nearly every geologic and natural form found along the entire Oregon Coast. The park is named after Cape Lookout, a rocky headland that juts out 2 miles into the sea. The slightly hilly walk out to the tip of the cape transports the visitor through dense stands of Silka spruce; into moist, shadowy glens and meadows brilliant with wildflowers in season; underneath monstrous trees bowled over by winter gales; and around corners that suddenly reveal exhilarating views of the sea and cape. The hike is easy and diverse enough to be of interest even to small children. In places however, it's best to hold on to all the little hands, as the trail comes skittishly close to steep drop-offs. Naturally, fearless young trekkers are unfazed by these "dangers."

A somber note to this otherwise attractive trek out the cape is a memorial marking the spot where a B-17 bomber crashed in 1943. The plane was patrolling the coast when it became lost in heavy fog and crashed into the cape, killing the entire crew. And, if you listen carefully you'll hear the eerie sounds of fog horns in the distance warning sailors of the dangerous rocks near the shore. In addition, Cape Lookout State Park offers day users such facilities as restrooms, drinking water, picnic sites, and a large shelter. Overnighters will find 250 campsites (53 full hookups), fireplaces, restrooms with showers, and drinking water.

Cape Meares State Park

Location: Three Capes Scenic Look, 9 miles northwest of Tillamook

This day use state park features stunning views, picnic sites, restrooms, and several easy trails that lead to natural attractions certain to delight young travelers. Two paved paths lead to the cliff-top perch of the Cape Meares Lighthouse. Though withdrawn from duty in 1963, the lighthouse was completely restored and is now open to visitors. Youngsters love to race up the spiral staircase in the tower for a peek at the huge prismatic Fresnel lenses. There's also an interesting historic collection of lighthouse-related artifacts and photos on the main level. Be sure to bring binoculars. The lighthouse provides excellent views of offshore wildlife at home on the Cape Meares Rocks. Children love the sight of so many seals, sea lions, cormorants, puffins, and other marine life lounging around in their natural habitat.

Another trail leads to an eerie natural phenomenon known as the Octopus Tree (see description in this chapter). This Sitka spruce of unusual size and shape lies just a short hike away from the lighthouse. A little farther on one can encounter yet another awesome spruce. This 193-foot Sitka has a trunk nearly 40 feet around and is thought to be over 400 years old. With so much of interest here, it's no wonder that the park is a perennial choice for so many family outings.

Annual Events

Autumn Festival and Sandcastle Contest

Location: Rockaway Beach State Park, off Hwy 101, Rockaway
Date: Third weekend in September
Phone: (800) 331–5928 or 355–8108

A huge bonfire on the beach Friday night kicks off this harvest time celebration. Younger children will love to gather with Mom and Dad under a warm, snugly blanket as the flickering flames cast eerie shadows all about. Sandcastle builders, young and old alike, gather early Saturday morning to start their sand sculptures. Judging usually takes place in the early afternoon, tides permitting. It's a playful event for kids as well as for grown-ups. Throughout the weekend the town of Rockaway Beach is the scene of live jazz and other entertainment. Food booths, games, and contests, plus a fabulous array of arts and crafts events and booths, are available in town. Craftspeople demonstrate their skills in creating articles ranging from ceramics and cloth puppets to wooden toys and leaded glass.

Dairy Festival and County Rodeo

Location: Downtown Tillamook and Fairgrounds
Date: Fourth weekend in June
Phone: 842–7525

Since 1958, this biggest little show on the Oregon Coast has been entertaining young and old alike with a variety of old-fashioned hometown fun events. Parades, western crafts demonstrations, exotic ethnic and down-home vittles, and roving rodeo clowns are but a few of the offerings you'll find here. Now for the real action. The perennial favorites on every youngster's must-see list are the bull riding, steer wrestling, and steer roping events that turn the rodeo arena into a thundering arena of man vs. beast.

Dory Festival

Location: Various locations in Pacific City, 17 miles southwest of Tillamook
Date: Third weekend in July
Phone: 965-6161

Each year the Dory Festival pays homage to a century-old tradition that has endured in this small community. The calm surf north of town has long provided a perfect launch for the double-ended, flat-bottomed boats developed by the sea's pioneer dory builders. The revelry begins with a colorful dory parade winding its way through Pacific City. Dory boat events include races with old-style oared dories as well as power dories. From their beach-side seats, kids will whoop it up as dorymen launch their vessels through the surf out to sea. It's a treat for the whole family to watch the dory crews compete in a series of grueling events designed to test their seafaring skills. Activities continue all weekend in town and include crafts booths and demonstrations, a fun run, dancing, and a low-cost fish fry—a complete meal with all the fish you can eat.

Rockaway Beach Kite Festival

Location: Rockaway Beach State Park, off Hwy 101, Rockaway
Date: Third weekend in May
Phone: (800) 331-5928 or 355-2995

Kite flyers and rubberneckers galore have been dropping by this beach since 1977 to take part in Rockaway's annual kite spectacular. Festivities get under way with a stirring evening exhibition of lighted kites. Kids love hunkering down on the dark, windswept beach while overhead sparks shower the night sky. With the return of day comes a variety of competitive events for all age groups. Among these are Indian fighter kite matches, rokkaku battles, teddy-bear drops, and single-string kite flying contests. For those wishing to challenge any world records, cash prizes are offered for the largest and smallest kites, and largest stack, wind tube, and wind sock. The final day's fare features a thrilling demonstration of hang gliders and iridescent hot-air balloons. It's a terrific finale.

Tillamook County Fair

Location: Fairgrounds, Tillamook
Date: Second week in August
Phone: 842–7525

For over 75 years families have been gathering here to enjoy this all-American traditional county fair. It's an event with lots to appeal to the kids, including agricultural and scientific exhibits, carnival rides, arts and crafts demonstrations, and an unusual auto racing event called the "Pig-N-Ford." Drivers speed along the course while grappling with a feisty pig in the front seat. A real side-splitter for adults and children alike.

Section 2
Central Oregon Coast

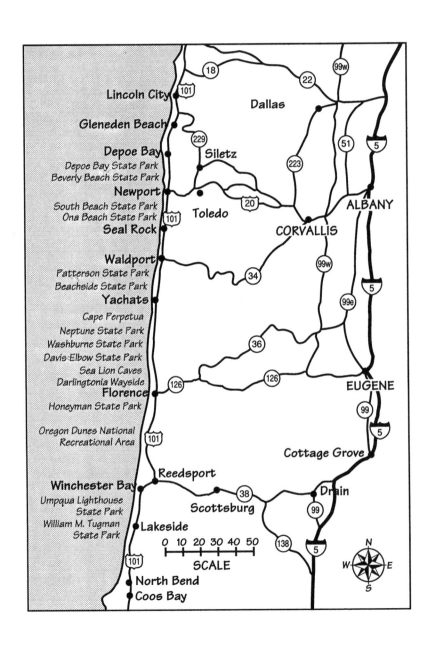

Lincoln City

Gleneden Beach

Depoe Bay
Depoe Bay State Park
Beverly Beach State Park

Newport
South Beach State Park
Ona Beach State Park
Seal Rock

Waldport
Patterson State Park
Beachside State Park

Yachats
Cape Perpetua
Neptune State Park
Washburne State Park
Davis Elbow State Park
Sea Lion Caves
Darlingtonia Wayside
Florence
Honeyman State Park

Oregon Dunes National
Recreational Area

Reedsport

Winchester Bay
Umpqua Lighthouse
State Park
William M. Tugman
State Park

Lakeside

North Bend

Coos Bay

Dallas

Siletz

Toledo

CORVALLIS

ALBANY

EUGENE

Cottage Grove

Scottsburg

Drain

0 10 20 30 40 50
SCALE

N
W · E
S

5

LINCOLN CITY

More than a quarter century ago, five small towns banded together to form a city that was to be named after America's sixteenth president. This popular family resort area offers visitors nearly every possible convenience and accommodation. Lincoln City boasts over 2,000 rooms with a view, and more shops, boutiques, and factory outlet stores than found in cities many times its size—all the while managing to retain its natural beauty and unspoiled charm. Recreational opportunities are in abundant supply. The public beach, which stretches nearly eight miles, seems to have been created for kite-flying. And anglers never tire of the challenges provided by the nearby ocean, rivers, and lakes.

Sights and Attractions

Abraham Lincoln Memorial
Location: N. E. 22nd and Quay, Lincoln City
Over 25 years ago, sculptress Anna Huntington donated an impressive 14-foot statue to the city. The four ton bronze statue of Abraham Lincoln reading a book while astride a

grazing horse was dedicated by then—Governor Mark Hatfield, poet Carl Sandburg, and actor Raymond Massey. Older children will be delighted to imagine the arduous journey Old Abe had to make just to get here. Because of its unusual size, the statue had to be shipped by barge from its casting in New Jersey to New York. Then, loaded aboard a rail car, the statue headed west to Chicago.

Just past Chicago, the huge bronze was placed aboard a trailer and routed through Canada. It seems that America's highway tunnels and overpasses were not high enough for Old Abe to squeeze through (after all, he was a tall president). Reaching Canada's west coast, the truck turned south, proceeding through Washington and Oregon to deposit its troublesome cargo at Lincoln City. Ever since its dedication however, the statue has been at the mercy of the elements and now sports a coat of green caused by oxidation of the bronze.

Blue Heron Landing

Location: 4006 W. Devil's Lake Rd., Lincoln City
Phone: 994–4708
Days/Hours: Daily 9–dusk
Cost: Varies by equipment

Devil's Lake, just east of Lincoln city, is a long, curved, freshwater body. It's ideal for all sorts of water recreation available to those intrepid sailors not fazed by the legends of a sea monster lurking there. On the lake, Blue Heron Landing offers a whole range of "wet-n-wild" rental equipment to better enjoy the peaceful lake waters. Virtually every sort of seaworthy vessel can be rented, including canoes, bumper boats, paddle boats, and motorboats. Before heading home, why not take an aqua bike out on the lake? These oversized tricycles come with huge balloon tires that let you stay afloat as you pedal around. The kids will love it, and so will the grown-ups. But please don't forget about the mythological behemoth residing in the lake. After all, it could be following your every splash.

Cascade Head Scenic Area

Location: Off Hwy 101 at Three Rocks Rd., 4 miles north of Lincoln City

Days/Hours: Daily, dawn to dusk

The Nature Conservancy Trail and the other trails on this land privately owned by the Nature Conservancy are open to public enjoyment. The Nature Conservancy Trail, about two miles long, begins in a coastal forest and leads to a grassy headland remarkable for its views of rivers, distant hills, and the ocean far below. It's an invigorating two-hour walk that even young explorers will treasure. Before starting out on any of the trails, be sure to pick up brochures at the trailheads describing the geography, ecology, and views of the surrounding area. Hand over the trail chart to the youngsters and let them plot the course. They'll love playing navigator — and learn a bit about map reading, to boot.

Catch the Wind

Location: 266 S.E. Hwy 101, Lincoln City

Phone: 994–9500

Days/Hours: Daily 9:30–5

Catch the Wind is packed to the rafters with kites, spin socks, and colorful creations of nearly every known size, shape, and color. It's a popular shop with kite flyers of all ages. And where better to locate their eight world famous Catch the Wind kite shops than along the Oregon Coast? Lying mid-way between the equator and North Pole, these beach cities are visited by predictably perfect winds for kites to catch. Other Catch the Wind shops are located in Seaside, Cannon Beach, Rockaway Beach, Depoe Bay, Agate Beach, Newport, and Florence.

North Lincoln County Museum

Location: 1512 S.E. Hwy 101, Lincoln City

Phone: 996–6614

Days/Hours: Wed–Sat 12–4

Cost: Free

On display are the everyday tools, furniture, and household utensils once used by the early seacoast homesteaders. Several scenes, filled with period artifacts and memorabilia, re-create an early pioneer kitchen, bedroom, and classroom. Children will enjoy seeing and touching the many fine relics, including a music organ, a large spinning wheel, and the handmade furniture. Native American pieces, and logging tools and equipment round out the museum's historical collection. This wonderful museum will instill in even the younger visitors a sense of the hard times faced by early settlers and of their American ingenuity that helped them survive and prosper.

Larry's Putt-A-Round

Location: 1255 N.W. Hwy 101, Lincoln City
Phone: 994–7888
Days/Hours: Tues–Thurs 4–9, Fri 4–11, Sat 10–11, Sun 11–9
Cost: $3/per player
Lincoln City's newest family indoor recreational activity features a 16 hole miniature golf course set against a coastal theme backdrop. Centrally located, Larry's Putt-A-Round invites residents and tourists alike to, in Larry's words: "come join the fun."

"Saturdays"

Location: At Devils Lake Golf & Racquet Club, 3245 Clubhouse Dr., Lincoln City
Phone: 996–3960
Days/Hours: Saturdays 8–11pm
Cost: $3/ages 13–21
Every Saturday night teens flock here in droves to spend an action-filled evening dancing, playing tennis, racquetball, ping pong, foosball, and pool. For those with less energy to burn off, there's a featured movie each week, board and card games, and Nintendo. Contests are held in various activities and the winners receive teen-oriented prizes such as stereos, cameras, boom boxes, watches, and cash. "Saturdays" prides itself on providing wholesome, pleasureful activities, free of drugs, alcohol, and cigarettes, for the young set lookin' for somethin' to do Saturday night.

Sitka Center for Art and Ecology
Location: Three Rocks Rd., Otis (7 miles north of Lincoln City)
Phone: 994–5485
This remarkable learning center, situated atop a bluff over-looking the sea, conducts an exciting summer program of weekend workshops and weeklong classes for adults and children on the art, music, and ecology of the Oregon Coast. Hands-on sessions in painting, drawing, ceramics, fibers, ecology, music, photography, and writing can be especially rewarding for older, imaginative children. A variety of entertaining evening happenings includes concerts, lectures, slide shows, and films. More information can be obtained by calling, or writing, Sitka Center for Art and Ecology, P.O. Box 65, Otis, Oregon 97368.

Tidepooling
Location: Various locations in Lincoln City
There's no better time than low tide to explore Lincoln City's many tidepools. Several beach accesses around town offer visitors a fascinating glimpse into a rarely seen undersea world–one that teems with a considerable variety of sea creatures. Tidepooling is a wonderful family activity that even the youngest explorers will love. Some of the best access spots are those at N.W. 15th St., at Canyon Dr. Park on S.W. 11th St., just off S.W. 35th St., and at the very north end of Roads End. But please remember to watch the tide. When it starts to return, it's time for you to retreat, and stay close to the younger members of your group at all times.

Quality Factory Village
Location: On Hwy 101 at East Devils Lake Rd., Lincoln City
Phone: 996–5000
Days/Hours: Mon–Sat 9:30–8, Sun 9:30–6
Nearly every member of the family will enjoy browsing at the forty-seven factory outlet stores at Quality Factory Village — Oregon's largest factory outlet mall. Name brand toys, clothing, shoes, as well as fashion accessories, books, and sweets, all at up to 70% off regular retail, await shoppers of all ages. While

not all the stores will interest the kids, a few do their best—and usually succeed—to corral the youngsters. They include Oshkosh B'Gosh (sportswear), Polly Flinders ("world famous Polly Flinders dresses"), Toy Liquidators (name brand toys), and The Paper Factory (party needs and games).

Parks and Camping

D River State Wayside

Location: Hwy 101, Lincoln City

Perched on a shelf overlooking the ocean, with fine grassy lawns and access to miles of clean, sandy beach, D River Wayside is a great family destination. Its midtown location makes it attractively close to most of Lincoln City's other sights and services. Although it might be easy to miss, be sure not to overlook the park's D River which connects the ocean with Devil's Lake. The river is reputed to be the world's shortest at a mere several hundred feet in length. The older children are usually fascinated by such claims to fame and can't wait to look it up in the Guiness Book of Records.

East Devil's Lake State Park

Location: East Devil's Lake Rd., 2 miles east of Lincoln City

Adjoining part of 2.5 mile long Devil's Lake, this popular day use park provides two attractive picnic areas, shelters, and restrooms. The lake's relatively warm temperature in summer makes the designated swimming beach here a great swimming hole for kids. There's also a boat launch and docks as well as several short, paved trails. Windsurfers and paddleboaters can rent the necessary rigs from several nearby equipment rental firms. Besides being home to a fabled sea monster, Devil's Lake provides fishermen with such popular catches as trout, bass, catfish, and perch.

Lincoln City Parks

Kirtsis Park

Location: Quay Ave. at 21st St., Lincoln City

This nice little park has a playground, several well-maintained picnic shelters, and restrooms. It's a good place to stop for a picnic if you're travelling.

Regatta Grounds Park

Location: On Devil's Lake, about .75 miles east of Hwy 101, Lincoln City

A park that has something for everyone, including a .5 mile jogging trail with exercise stations, play equipment, picnic tables, and restrooms. This well-groomed park has plenty of room for youngsters to run, play, or just explore. It's a great spot to spend a few hours.

Wecoma Park

Location: Jetty Ave. at 31st St., Lincoln City

Now's the time to get the basketball or volleyball out of the trunk. The kids will enjoy playing on the hard surface courts. One court has the basketball hoops; the other, a volleyball net. There are also restrooms and a playground for smaller children.

Neskowin Beach State Park

Location: Hawk St. in Neskowin, 9 miles north of Lincoln City

The locals don't like to crow about this hideaway for fear of letting the secret out. On sunny, weekend afternoons when all of Lincoln City's beach parks are virtually packed to the rafters, "insiders" head to Neskowin Beach State Park. The views are gorgeous, the beaches are a young beachcomber's delight, and the serene garden-like landscape will soothe the nerves of even the most stressed-out traveller. And with restrooms and drinking water available, Neskowin is a perfect spot for the whole family to spend a few hours or longer.

Road's End Wayside

Location: West of Lighthouse Square Shopping Center, Lincoln City

This is another one of those gems known to only a few. While the hordes are packing many of Lincoln City's other beaches, the Road's End Wayside is often amazingly overlooked. Kids love exploring the wayside's remarkable tidepools as well as poking around the fine beach carpet of pebbles and rocks in search of agate specimens. The really adventurous wait until the tide is out, then hike around the headland to investigate a part of the beach that few get to see. Incidentally, beating a hasty retreat as soon as the tide turns is not only mandatory for safety, it's also an activity most kids find exciting.

West Devil's Lake State Park

Location: 1452 N.E. 6th Dr., Lincoln City
Phone: 994–2002
Days/Hours: Mid–April thru late October
Cost: Free/day use, $9–13/camping

Most visitors are pleasantly surprised to discover that such an excellent full-service public campground is so close to the heart of Lincoln City's tourist center. This state campground offers 100 campsites, which include 68 tent and 32 full hookup sites. Solar showers, boat moorages, and a hiker-biker campground round out the facilities.

The park is literally a stone's throw from both Devil's Lake, a large body of freshwater, and the ocean, just across the highway. Several nearby companies rent canoes, paddleboats, and bumper boats to young explorers who hope to be the first in modern times to find the mythological sea monster that inhabits the lake. Fishing, windsurfing, swimming, and hydroplaning are a few of the other recreational opportunities available here.

Annual Events

International Fall Kite Festival
Location: D River Wayside, Lincoln City
Phone: (800) 452–2151 or 994–3070
Date: Last weekend in September
Since 1978, Oregon's largest kite festival has been attracting kite flyers from Asia, Europe, and all over North America. It's a terrific event for children to watch. The skydivers, team-kite choreography, and lighted kite night fly are absolutely dazzling. A variety of contests are held throughout the festival, the most awesome of which is the kite battle. The kids will cheer as the combatants in this traditional, Japanese-style fight try to tangle or knock their opponents' kites out of the sky.

Grass Carp Festival
Location: Devil's Lake, Lincoln City
Phone: (800) 452–2151 or 994–3070
Date: First weekend in September
When an overgrowth of weeds in Devil's Lake completely choked off recreation, grass carp were introduced to rid the lake of these pesky plants. In practically no time, the carp devoured the weeds, and the lake was once again a recreation site. Since 1986, the annual Grass Carp Festival has been honoring the carp and celebrating the re-birth of the lake. This sensational event has something for every member of the family. Festivities include a dazzling, colorful display of water ski choreography by the Rose City Ski Team, canoe races, a 5K foot race, and lake cruises. Whether they just watch or actually join in, youngsters will delight in the children's games and contests. There's even a playground for keeping the really young ones happy. A local jazz band provides the perfect musical accompaniment for this delightful event.

Spring Kite Festival

Location: D River Wayside, Lincoln City
Date: Second weekend in May
Phone: (800) 452–2151 or 994–3070

Each spring since 1983, the skies above this vast sandy beach are illuminated with all the splendid sights and sounds of a kite-flying extravaganza. Pros and newcomers alike compete in a wide range of contests (though the promoters claim the Spring Kite Festival is the most laid back of all coastal kite-flying events). The children especially will be delighted by the many innovative, humorous, and just plain spectacular sky displays—including some multi-colored, colossal "spin socks" that are nearly 50 yards long. Just after dusk, lighted kites are sent skyward, providing the effect of fireflies swarming against a pitch-black celestial background. It's a wonderful, enchanting sight that will warm the hearts of all.

6

DEPOE BAY

The six acre postage stamp harbor at Depoe Bay is the world's tiniest, natural, navigable harbor. Its narrow channel and deep water make it the best protected bay on the Oregon Coast. A U.S. Coast Guard base as well as a flourishing fleet of commercial, charter, private fishing, and sightseeing boats call Depoe Bay "home." Natural wonders abound here. This resort community is fortunate to be situated along one of the most beautiful stretches of coastline to be found anywhere. Near Depoe Bay, along Highway 101, several state parks offer spectacular views of the coast. Next to the harbor, a historical marker describes the town's background including the story of how it got its name from Charlie Depoe, a Rogue River Indian, who in his youth had worked at a nearby U.S. Army depot.

Sights and Attractions

Alder House II

Location: .75 miles east on Immonen Rd., Gleneden Beach
Phone: 996–2483
Days/Hours: Daily 10–5

A geodesic dome, peacefully surrounded by an alder grove, sits a short distance from Siletz Bay. Within this unusual setting, a glass blower's studio turns molten glass into a wide variety of top quality practical and artistic glassware, including vases, bowls, paperweights, and goblets. Youngsters will be captivated as they watch the glass blowers twirling and shaping the fiery blobs of molten glass at the ends of their long hollow tubes. Expect more than one youthful chorus of "ooh" and "aah" as identifiable shapes begin to emerge from the hot lumps of glass.

Cape Foulweather

Location: On the Otter Crest Loop, south of Depoe Bay

Discovered and named by the famed English explorer, James Cook, in the midst of a vicious storm, Cape Foulweather affords spectacular, panoramic ocean views. When the weather is clear, you can easily see distances of 30 to 40 miles in all directions. On the other hand, you won't "almost see forever" when one of the Cape's typical foul weather winter storms ushers in 50 mile per hour gales. Sometimes fog will quickly descend, enveloping the area in a thick smoky gray that will all but obliterate the view past your nose. Off the parking lot, there's a fenced pathway that the kids will thrill to race along. On both sides are steep, forested cliffs that sweep menacingly toward the sea far below. At the end of the path, a telescope allows youngsters to peek out at distant ships and at sea lions that sunbathe on the offshore rocks at low tide.

Depoe Bay Aquarium

Location: Hwy 101 and Bay St., Depoe Bay
Phone: 765–2259
Days/Hours: Daily 10–8 (summer), 10–5 (rest of year)
Cost: $2.25/adults, $1.75/ages 6–11, free/5 years and under
Entering this aquarium, one of America's oldest, is like being transported to a huge, undersea cave. As kids peer through rock framed windows, a dazzling, often bizarre array of marine life zips in and out of view. In another section of the museum, a gigantic tank is home to a small herd of California sea lions and harbor seals. These entertaining creatures are born hams who've learned all the necessary tricks to get the delighted youngsters to toss them bits of fish. A few other crowd pleasers include: a quarter-ton green sea turtle, a ferocious wolf eel, and several octopuses that can change skin color from deep red to white in a jiffy.

Marine Gardens

Location: Off B St. in Otter Rock
The best time to bring the youngsters here is at low tide when the pools and caves offer an excellent, albeit temporary, look at sea urchins, starfish, anemones, and other colorful tidepool inhabitants. In addition to the B Street entrance, access to Marine Gardens can also be made during low tide along the trail from the north side of nearby Devil's Punchbowl State Park.

Mossy Creek Pottery

Location: .5 miles east of Hwy 101 on Immonen Rd., Gleneden Beach
Phone: 996–2415
Days/Hours: Daily 10–5
A charming roadside cottage in a woodsy setting houses this unique pottery workshop and gallery. Even small children will be fascinated to watch master potters busily at work on fine hand-thrown porcelain and stoneware. With prices on the shop's high-quality creations being much lower than at typi-

cal urban pottery outlets, many sharp shoppers have been known to snap up quite a few bargains.

Otter Crest Loop

Location: On the heights between Depoe Bay and Newport Otter Crest Loop is a beautiful, scenic road that every visitor to the Oregon Coast should experience. Part of the old Oregon Highway, this five-mile excursion starts out along the lower coastal cliffs and provides views of pounding surf and secluded beaches from between dense stands of fir and spruce. The loop curves, then continues to climb—at times ticklishly close to the sheer cliffs nearly 500 feet above the sea—until reaching its summit at Cape Foulweather. The kids may love every moment the road comes perilously close to the edge, but it's the sort of roller coaster ride that will make some drivers skittish .

Salishan

Location: On Hwy 101, Gleneden Beach
Phone: (800) 452–2300 or 764–3600
This nationally acclaimed five star resort offers its guests a veritable grab bag of fun things to do. While the adults are having a workout on Salishan's Championship golf course, tennis facilities, pool, whirlpool, sauna, fitness center, or jogging track, the kids will have plenty of options as well. A video game arcade complex, playground with swings, teeter-totter, sandbox, climbing equipment, nature trails, and a private beach all add up to plenty of action-filled time. Older youngsters will especially enjoy whacking away at the buckets of golf balls available at the golf course. And even if you're just passing through town, Salishan makes a great "pit stop." The restrooms are large and impeccably maintained; the restaurant's food outstanding. And there's absolutely no charge for travellers to wander through the art gallery or hike Salishan's forested trails.

The Spouting Horns

Location: Along the seawall north of Depoe Bay's harbor

Although not as regular as Old Faithful of Yellowstone National Park, Depoe Bay's Spouting Horns are every bit as spectacular. The spouting horns are natural rock formations in the cliffs along the waterfront that flood with the incoming tides and blast sea water high into the air, squirting arches across the highway. It's an awesome, natural spectacle that'll rivet the attention of even the youngest children. Although there's no way of telling when these geyser eruptions may occur, they're at their best in winter when ocean storms throw the tides into the cliffs with quite a wallop.

Sunset Scenic Flights

Location: Hangar #7, Gleneden Beach State Airport
Phone: 764–3304
Days/Hours: Call for hours, reservations required
Cost: $50/3 adults or 2 adults & 2 small children

Taking off from Gleneden Beach, the small Cessna Skylane climbs to around 1,800 feet for the cruise between Newport and Lincoln City. Young noses press against the glass, searching for migrating whales far below. These delightful 30 minute flights cover about 70 miles of ocean and coastline.

Thundering Seas

Location: On South Point Road, about one-half mile south of Depoe Bay Bridge
Phone: 765–2604

Thundering Seas is a distinguished school for the training of gold and silversmiths. Kids and grown-ups will enjoy observing students working with precious metals as they fabricate jewelry, flatware, ornaments, and table sculpture. Visitors are welcome to take an interesting tour of the rest of the school, workshops, and mineral display room. Call for tour information and group arrangements.

United States Coast Guard Station

Location: On east side of harbor, Depoe Bay
Days/Hours: Mon–Sat 4–8 pm, Sun 1–8 pm

The Coast Guard's search and rescue station plays a vital role in insuring a safe maritime environment for coastal residents and visitors alike. Its "fleet" consists of two 44-foot motorized lifeboats, a 30-foot surf rescue boat, and an inflatable life raft. These are some of the things youngsters will get to see while touring the station. Visitors who time it right get to watch Coast Guard personnel running through their training exercises to fine-tune the skills they must use in emergency and stormy conditions. It's a drill that everyone, regardless of age, will find fascinating.

Whale Watching Cruises

See introduction to "Whale Watching Cruises" in Chapter 7.

Depoe Bay Sportfishing

Location: South end of bridge, Depoe Bay
Phone: 765-2222
Days/Hours: Call for hours
Cost: $8/adults, $6/ages 9–18, free/8 and under

Operates daily one hour cruises in summer, less often at other times. Sightseeing trips and evening tours are available for groups and individuals. Reservations recommended, but not required.

Dockside Charters

Location: On Bay St., near the Coast Guard Station at Depoe Harbor
Phone: 765-2545
Days/Hours: Call for hours
Cost: $8/adults, $6/ages 12 and under

Runs hourly trips on a daily basis, year round, but less often when sightings are at a minimum. Reservations suggested.

Tradewinds Ocean Sport Fishing
Location: On Hwy 101 at north end of bridge at Depoe Bay
Phone: 765–2345
Days/Hours: Call for hours
Cost: $8/adults, $6/ages 12 and under
Operates hourly cruises on a daily basis from mid-December to mid-January and again from March through May. Call for schedule for all other times. Reservations required.

Parks and Camping

Beverly Beach State Park
Location: On Hwy 101, 6.5 miles south of Depoe Bay
Phone: 265–9278
Cost: Free/day use, $11–13/camping
Long a family favorite with many Oregonians, Beverly Beach State Park reposes in a lush forest on Spencer Creek, not far from the ocean beaches. It's both a day-use and overnight camping facility featuring 279 campsites (tent, electrical, and full hook-up sites). Young beachcombers can forage along the shoreline, while older youngsters may prefer to explore the forested setting surrounding the campground or swim in either the ocean or creek. In summer, the park's amphitheater is the scene of evening slide shows that are geared for the entire family. The only fly in the ointment is the small parking lot which discourages the day-use visitor on crowded weekends. Early reservations are suggested.

Boiler Bay State Park
Location: On Hwy 101, 1 mile north of Depoe Bay
Disasters at sea always seem to capture our attention. Not far off shore, over 80 years ago, the steam schooner Marhoffer burst into flames when a gas torch ignited in the engine room. Lifeboats were launched as the blazing ship, in the grip of the incoming tide, headed toward shore where it crashed and

blew apart. Although all of the crew members survived, only the ship's boiler remained intact, washing ashore and embedding itself in the sand. Nowadays, when the tide is low, young shipwreck buffs can wander out to the old boiler for a first hand examination—which usually includes plenty of climbing and jumping. The park's picnic sites, restrooms, and splendid ocean views make this a truly lovely place for a family outing.

Devil's Punch Bowl State Park

Location: On Hwy 101, 4 miles south of Depoe Bay

The "punch bowl" was formed when the roof fell in on two adjoining sea caves. During high tide, water rushes in with a roar and crashes against the cavern walls, spewing foam in every direction. It's a thrilling demonstration of nature's awesome strength. When the tide is out, the punch bowl is empty and quiet—although the bare cavern is still well worth a look. This day use state park also features picnic sites with ocean views and long, clean stretches of sandy beach, as well as tidepools and a scattering of grottos that kids will love to explore.

Fogarty Creek State Park

Location: On Hwy 101, 2 miles north of Depoe Bay

Nestled in a tiny canyon, Fogarty Creek State park offers day users several spacious picnic areas and shelters, restrooms, drinking water, and lots of parking space. The park adjoins a small crystal-clear stream that empties into a sheltered cove, making an idyllic site for fishing, picnicking, and especially beachcombing. Since there's enough protection here from the wind, it's also a great spot for sunbathing.

Rocky Creek State Park

Location: Off Hwy 101, 2 miles south of Depoe Bay

This attractive day-use park offers visitors several small picnic areas, restrooms, water, and a striking blufftop location overlooking the ocean. Armed with binoculars, whale watchers have a good perch here for catching fleeting glimpses of the gentle, migrating, behemoths. Rocky Creek's large, flat terrain contains many well-mown lawns that are perfect "run and play" areas.

Annual Events

The Fleet of Flowers
Location: Harbor at Depoe Bay
Date: Memorial Day
Phone: 765–2889
After special harborside services, memorial wreaths and bouquets are loaded aboard small boats for a somber trip out to sea. With Coast Guard vessels in the lead, a flotilla of nearly 50 ships slowly heads through the rocky channel and out to sea to pay tribute to those area residents who have been lost at sea. Beyond the channel, the flowers and wreaths are cast upon the waters as the ships parade in a circle around the ever-expanding carpet of blossoms. It's a beautiful, bittersweet, traditional event that touches the hearts.

Indian Salmon Bake
Location: At Fogarty State Park, on Hwy 101 north of Depoe Bay
Date: Third Sat in September, 11–4
Phone: 765–2889
Depoe Bay's population of several hundred swells to nearly 5,000 when the community's annual salmon bake, first held in 1956, arrives in late September. About 2,500 pounds of fresh salmon are baked (early-Indian style) on the beach on Alder stakes thrust into the sand over open fire trenches. It's an interesting cookout, especially for older children, made more so by the presence of a live band and strolling clowns.

7

NEWPORT

For over a century, tourism has been a major industry in this fishing port at the mouth of the Yaquina River. Newport's galleries, boutiques, and eateries that line the historic bay front district attract visitors from Canada to Mexico. No town between San Francisco and Seattle offers travellers more oceanfront hotel rooms than Newport. Fishing, crabbing, and clamming are popular recreational pursuits as well as serious commercial activities here. Have no doubts that Newport is a genuine seaport where huge commercial trawlers ply the same waters of Yaquina Bay as does a mini-fleet of charter and rental boats. Canneries and packing houses dominate the wharves with their bustling activity as fresh seafood is cleaned, crated, loaded, and delivered to markets around the country.

Sights and Attractions

The Belle of Newport

Location: On the Bayfront in Newport
Phone: 265–2355
Hours: 11:30 am & 1:30 pm, plus dinner cruises
Cost: $10/adults, $5/under 5

While cruising Yaquina Bay aboard The Belle of Newport, you'll be treated to views of sea lions and seals that you just don't see from land. And your youngsters will be captivated by these close-ups of wildlife at home in their natural habitat. The Belle, a smaller version of the old time Mississippi riverboat, is complete with a player piano, live entertainment, a full snack bar, and sternwheeler paddles that actually do propel her. It's a fun ship the kids will love to explore. On your excursion, you'll also get a close-up look at seafood processing facilities, ships off-loading their catches, the dramatic Yaquina Bay Bridge, ship loading terminals, and many types of commercial and pleasure craft. As many will agree, there's nothing quite like 90 minutes of sightseeing from the decks of a genuine sternwheeler. Also, chartering the vessel for a wedding, anniversary, or birthday can make for quite a memorable event.

Bertea Aviation Scenic Flights

Location: 3 miles south at Newport Municipal Airport
Phone: 867–7767
Days/Hours: Daily 8–6 (summer), 8–5 (winter)
Cost: $25/person

Bertea Aviation offers airplane rides aboard their Cessna 172 (high wing, four seater) over the coast from Newport to Cape Perpetua or in the opposite direction toward Lincoln City. The trip lasts about thirty minutes and involves some remarkably scenic flying over coastal forest, rivers, and lakes. It's a terrific opportunity for kids to gain a different perspective of the coastal topography. Reservations are required. The aircraft holds up to three passengers. *Note:* With two paying adults aboard the same flight, a child under 12 can fly free of charge.

Electric Beach

Location: 424 South Coast Hwy, Newport
Phone: 265–2200
Days/Hours: Daily 10–10 (summer), 10–8 (winter)
Cost: $2.50/adults, $1.50/under 12 (miniature golf)

Visitors to this family entertainment complex, located in Newport's City Center, will find a variety of indoor attractions to choose from. The miniature golf course, with its electrical obstacles, will challenge any budding Arnold Palmer or Lee Trevino in your entourage. Besides golf, there are five pool tables, foosball, and a video game arcade that young and old alike will enjoy. A soda fountain and snack bar provide the necessary nourishment to keep up the action.

Hatfield Marine Science Center

Location: 2030 Marine Science Dr., south of Newport across
the Yaquina Bay Bridge
Phone: 867–0100
Days/Hours: Daily 10–6 (summer), 10–4 (rest of year)
Cost: Free

It's not every day you'll walk into a museum and be greeted by a large octopus who just could be having a meal at the time. The creature in the tank is quite gentle and actually has been known to reach out and touch visitors with his suction-tipped tentacles. Go ahead and give it a handshake. But don't expect it to share dinner with you. As you wander through the center, you'll see many fine displays featuring just about everything you might want to know about the natural history of the Oregon Coast. Aquarium tanks abound and are filled with some of the strangest sea life to be found inhabiting the ocean. Kids of all ages love to reach into the "touch and feel" tank for a first hand meeting with starfish, crabs, snails, sea anemones, sea urchins, and mollusks.

A reconstructed whale skeleton and jaw bones, a bookstore, tidepools teeming with sea creatures, and marine science films are some of the other features of the center. Starting the third week in June and ending Labor Day, Seatauqua, a cooperative program, features daily films, workshops, nature hikes, and much more of interest to young visitors. Of course, it's not all fun and games here. The Hatfield Marine Science Center is the keystone of Oregon State University's coastal research, teaching, and marine extension activities.

Lincoln County Historical Society Museums

Location: 545 S.W. 9th St., Newport
Phone: 996–6614
Days/Hours: Tues–Sun 11–4, 10–5 (summer)
Cost: Free

The Lincoln County Historical Society has amassed a wonderful collection, and houses it in two adjoining museums, the Burrows House and the Log Cabin. The Burrows House, built a century ago, was originally a boarding house, then a funeral home, and now a repository for pioneer artifacts and history including household furnishings, clothing, and lots of period antiques. There's also a wonderful little bookstore that's a pleasure to browse. In addition to a selection of books on local and period history, the reproductions of Victorian books for kids and Victorian greeting cards will not fail to delight young history buffs. The Log Cabin Museum was built in the 1960s mostly by volunteers with donated materials. Children will find the maritime exhibits (plenty of local shipwreck photos and flotsam) and homesteading and logging tools fascinating. The museum also contains an outstanding collection of Indian basketry and ceremonial items.

Newport Performing Arts Center

Location: 777 W. Olive, Newport
Phone: 265–ARTS
Cost: $5–7/adults, $3/kids, $15–20/families

The 400-seat Newport Performing Arts Center, the state's newest state-of-the-arts performing facility, draws upon local, regional, and national talent to showcase everything from jazz to Shakespeare. Designed with an intimacy that surrounds the audience, the Center offers a multitude of year round programs. The Family Series events are priced and scheduled with families in mind, offering such morsels as costumed Renaissance music performers; a mother and daughter folk singing duo; an opera humorously performed especially for teens and pre-teens; jugglers, clowns, and magicians performing vaudeville theater. The behind-the-scenes look at stages, dressing rooms, and sets is a favorite with kids. Just call ahead and arrange to be part of a guided tour.

Oregon Coast Aquarium
Location: 2820 S.E. Ferry Slip Rd., Newport
Phone: 867–3474
Days/Hours: Daily 9–6 (summer), 10–4:30 (winter)
Cost: $7/adults, $5/seniors & students, $3/children, free/ under 4 years
The Oregon Coast Aquarium lets visitors discover the most fascinating denizens of the sea in a spectacular way that no other "fish behind glass" aquarium ever could. Kids and grownups will enjoy a walk through the Aquarium's indoor exhibits where they'll see waves crashing on a beach, a sea weed forest swaying in the currents, and exotic fish darting to and fro through a coastal reef. A theater, devoted to whales, features a fascinating ten minute video on the leviathans. There's a bookstore and gift shop stocked with field guides, marine books, and educational toys and products. Outdoors, elaborately rocked and landscaped cliffs, bluffs, beaches, and a fog-shrouded forest provide a dramatic habitat for sea otters, seals, sea lions, and other marine creatures. A walk-through aviary, complete with marine birds, a sandy beach, and gurgling tidepools, will fascinate the young set.

Ripley's—Believe It or Not
Location: 250 S.W. Bay Blvd., Mariner Square, Newport
Phone: 265–2206
Days/Hours: Daily 9–8 (summer), 10–5 (rest of year)
Cost: $5/adults, $3/ages 12–17, $2/ages 5–11
You'll really have to see some of these things to believe them. Brace yourself, then drop in on the accursed King Tut's Tomb; hike through a creepy graveyard and meet a ghost; experience a severe earthquake; descend to the depths of the ocean floor

and explore the Titanic; come nose-to-nose with a real shrunken head; walk across a glowing bed of coals; meet a mummy. There's something for everyone here. When you feel your circuits starting to overload, why not just take Ripley's three-dimensional space walk among the stars? You'll think and feel as if you are millions of miles from earth.

Sea Towne Courtyard

Location: 1600 N. Hwy 101, Newport
Days/Hours: Daily 10–5
The twenty shops at Sea Towne are grouped around several beautifully landscaped courtyards. While not every store will appeal to kids, it's an attractive walk on both upper and lower shopping levels along covered wooden walkways. Some of the more unusual shopping opportunities include handcrafted gifts, a well-stocked bookstore, cards from around the world, a fabric boutique, and last but not least, a deli with scrumptious morsels for all. One shop specializes in educational materials and quality import toys—a favorite with children, as you'd expect. Sea Towne is not difficult to find. As you're heading north on the highway just look for the ship's mast with flags flying.

The Undersea Gardens

Location: 250 S.W. Bay Blvd., Mariner Square, Newport
Phone: 265–2206
Days/Hours: Daily 9–8 (summer), 10–5 (rest of year)
Cost: $5/adults, $3/ages 12–17, $2/ages 5–11
Your descent beneath the sea begins with a journey down a wide stairway. A glass-walled viewing chamber affords a view of several thousand marine creatures—some of them unbelievably strange. Kids will be captivated by the ferocious wolfeels, giant octopuses, and gargantuan barnacles that dwell here. With visitors comfortably nestled in their seats in the undersea theater, the curtain rolls back to show an action-packed performance featuring fully equipped scuba divers and some of the larger, more forbidding sea creatures that lurk in this submarine jungle.

United States Coast Guard Station Yaquina Bay

Location: At east end of Bay Blvd., on Newport's waterfront
Days/Hours: Daily 1–4
Sort of like visiting the neighborhood fire station, a tour of the U.S. Coast Guard Station at Yaquina Bay will provide an insider's look at how the U.S.C.G. carries out its marine search-and-rescue mission for ships in distress. It's interesting to watch and particularly educational for older children. In front of the station there's a memorial park honoring those who have died at sea. A 36-foot motor lifeboat, retired from active duty after many years of rescue work, sits in the center of the park.

The Wax Works

Location: 250 S.W. Bay Blvd., Mariner Square, Newport
Phone: 265–2206
Days/Hours: Daily 9–8 (summer), 10–5 (rest of year)
Cost: $5/adults, $3/ages 12–17, $2/ages 5–11
The Wax Works is a "living" wax museum where wax figures, some of whom literally are from out of this world, move, talk, disappear, then turn up again. The various chambers are inhabited by lifelike monsters, freaks, legends, and even well-known Hollywood celebrities. There's a swaying bridge to cross, a rain forest guarded by the legendary Big Foot, a cabaret filled with famous movie stars, and plenty of other sets designed to astonish and entertain the whole family.

Whale Watching Cruises

One of the planet's most interesting wildlife shows takes place along the Oregon Coast every year. From December to June, California gray whales can be seen making part of their 12,000 mile roundtrip migration between Baja, Mexico and the Arctic. After a summer of gluttony in Arctic waters, and with the approach of cold weather, thousands of gray whales head south to balmy Mexico, where the pregnant females will give birth to their calves. Gray whales average about five to seven miles per hour, and can be seen off the Oregon Coast on the southward leg of their journey from mid-December to February, and northward from March to June.

Although coastal headlands offer whale watchers some fine ringside seats, there's nothing quite as spectacular as being aboard a sightseeing boat steaming full speed ahead for a close up you'll never forget. It's not uncommon for one or more whales to rise out of the water, often showing up to three-fourths of their length, then crash down on their massive frames in a performance known as "breaching"—and the splash is awesome. Like a Greyhound bus doing a belly-flop.

Fish On

Location: Bay Blvd., Newport
Phone:265-8607
Days/Hours: Winter & spring afternoon departures by reservation only
Cost: $16/person
Runs two hour cruises, as well as bay tours, and other custom sightseeing cruises for groups.

Newport Sportfishing

Location: 1000 S.E. Bay Blvd., Newport
Phone: 265-7558
Days/Hours: Weekends 10 am & 1 pm (December thru April)
Cost: $20/adults, $10/under 12
Two hour cruises only. Reservations suggested.

Newport Tradewinds

Location: 653 S.W. Bay Blvd., Newport
Phone: 265-2101
Days/Hours: Daily 10 am & 1:30 pm (January thru June)
Cost: $18/adults, free/5 years and under
Offers two and one-half hour trips, weather permitting. Reservations suggested. Also, one and two hour bay and ocean excursions.

Oregon Natural Resources Council
Location: Embarcadero Dock, Newport
Phone: 223–9012
Days/Hours: Weekends 10 am & 1 pm (March & April)
Cost: $25/adults, $20/ages 12 and under
Offers two hour cruises which feature short, but informative whale-watching presentations.

Sea Gull Charters
Location: 343 S.W. Bay Blvd., Newport
Phone: 265–7441
Days/Hours: Call for days/hours (November thru May)
Cost: $14/person
Two hour cruises. Also one hour sightseeing and nature excursions.

South Beach Charters
Location: South Beach Marina, Newport
Phone: 867–7200
Days/Hours: Weekends 1 pm only (winter), Daily 1 pm only (spring)
Cost: $18/person
Operates two hour cruises, including custom sightseeing tours for large groups. Reservations suggested but will take walk-ins.

Yaquina Bay Lighthouse
Location: In Yaquina Bay State Park on the northwest side of the Yaquina Bay Bridge
Phone: 867–7451
Days/Hours: Daily 10–5 (summer), Sat & Sun 11–4 (winter)
Cost: 50¢
This lighthouse has a colorful, if not bizarre, past, if you believe all the stories. After only three years in service, the beacon was shut down in 1874. Apparently this site was a poor one for a lighthouse since its light could not be seen by ships coming from the north due to protruding headlands a few miles up the

coast. It was replaced by another lighthouse at Yaquina Head. There's more to this particular lighthouse, however. Not long after it was vacated, a young woman, visiting with friends, entered a small room within the abandoned lighthouse, and disappeared. Her friends heard a blood curdling scream, and raced to the room to find only a warm pool of blood. The woman was never seen again.

Nowadays, the lighthouse has been restored and is open to the public. A museum on the premises features period furniture, historical photographs, and a short video recounting the strange disappearance of the young visitor long ago. Although dismissed by experts, there have been many reports of strange happenings at the lighthouse. Several observers claimed to have spotted the young woman's ghost, and museum keepers over the years have been at a loss to explain sudden temperature changes within the building. Whether you believe in spirits or not, should you find yourself outside the lighthouse on a dark, mist-shrouded afternoon and hear a wild and weird shriek from within, don't loiter.

Parks and Camping

Pacific Shores RV Resort

Location: 6225 N. Hwy 101, just north of Hwy 20, Newport
Phone: 265–3750 or (800) 333–1583
Cost: $16–28/space (summer), $11–21/space (winter)

Just a stone's throw from crashing waves, rocky shores and soft, sandy beaches, Pacific Shores RV Resort is considered by many to be one of the finest RV parks on the West Coast. Its 287 spacious sites are surrounded by natural beauty and creature comforts at every turn. The kids will love the amenities here: a playground, cable T.V., lighted nature trails, large heated indoor pool, spa, sauna, billiard room, big screen T.V.s, and game room. And in summer, arts, crafts, and game activities are conducted daily.

South Beach State Park

Location: 2 miles south of Newport off Hwy 101
Phone: 867–4715
Days: Mid–April thru October
Cost: Free/day use, $12/camping

It's not hard to see why this is one of the Oregon coast's most popular family camping spots. Each of the park's 254 camp-sites has drinking water, electricity, picnic tables, and a fire-place (firewood is available for a fee). Two well developed picnic areas are found at the park's south end. One of these is in the open, with easy access to the wide, sandy beaches. The other is a bit farther back, behind a large forested dune which provides some protection when sea breezes get a bit pushy. There's plenty for kids and grown-ups to do here: beachcomb-ing, sunbathing, clam digging, agate hunting and hiking are a few of the fun possibilities. Thanks to its' easy access to nearby Yaquina Bay and Newport, this campground fills up quickly, so reserve early.

Yaquina Head Outstanding Natural Area

Location: 3 miles north of Newport off Hwy 101
Days/Hours: Daily, dawn to dusk

Fast becoming one of Newport's major visitor attractions, this 100 acre preserve provides a wealth of scenic, scientific, edu-cational, and recreational opportunities. Since Yaquina Head defiantly juts out into the Pacific, it takes quite a battering from the forces of nature. Interestingly, marine life flourishes in this seemingly hostile environment. A number of species of sea birds and harbor seals make this area their home as does an amazing variety of sea creatures residing in the many tidepools here. Kids love to take the stairway down the cliff for a first hand look at these tidepools or to head over to the observation deck for a peek through the telescope. In early winter and again in spring, gray whales can easily be seen as they migrate en masse along the coast. Although it's closed to the public, you can still marvel at the beauty of nearby Yaquina Head Lighthouse, Oregon's tallest (and still active) lighthouse.

Annual Events

Festival of Gems and Treasures

Location: 1125 S.W. Coast Hwy, just northeast of the Yaquina Bay Bridge, Newport
Date: First week in June, Daily 10–5
Phone: 265–6330

This annual festival of precious materials is always a "must see" for young rock hounds fascinated by unusual minerals, shells, corals, and fossils. The Gallery regularly stocks an enormous inventory of marine gems and treasures. Facets Gem and Mineral Gallery hosts this sparkling event and displays their splendid collection.

Fisherman's Harvest Festival

Location: Marina at South Beach, Newport
Date: Third weekend in October
Phone: 265–8801 or (800) 262–7844

Seafood enthusiasts will think they're in heaven at this autumn sea festival in Newport. And while the grown-ups are lining up at the wine tasting displays, the older kids will be attracted to the many unusual arts and crafts booths. For an added attraction, many of the artisans and craftspeople demonstrate their special talents. An assortment of delicacies and treats are available at food booths set up throughout the marina.

Loyalty Days and Sea Fair

Location: Citywide, Newport
Date: First Thurs thru Sun in May
Phone: 265–8801, or (800) 262–7844

In each of the past 35 years Newport has celebrated Loyalty Days and Sea Fair with a burst of sights, sounds, and pageantry that has delighted visitors of all ages. There's not a nook or cranny in Newport that won't be the scene of some special happening. Children will enjoy a flashy carnival that runs continuously throughout the celebration at South Beach, near the Hatfield Marine Science Center. And then there's the big parade on Saturday at noon starting at the north end of town. Just before the parade, there is a 2-K run along the parade route. While the Sea Fair Queen is crowned at the Performing Arts Center, Navy and Coast Guard ships drop anchor, inviting youngsters in for some exciting touring. Rounding out the festival are sailboat races, a vintage car show, an adult 1950s dance, and plenty of arts, crafts, and food booths.

Seafood and Wine Festival

Location: Marina at South Beach, Newport
Date: Last weekend in February
Phone: 265–8801, or (800) 262–7844
Cost: $3 entrance fee

Since 1977, people have been turning out in large numbers for this gala celebration—tens of thousands each year, in fact. Although the youngsters won't be involved with wine tasting, the food booths will feature a wide selection of fresh, local seafood that will certainly appeal to everyone's taste buds. This giant block party is made more festive by the addition of dozens of artists and craftspeople hawking their colorful wares. All this, and live music too, make Newport's Seafood and Wine Festival a premier coastal event.

8

WALDPORT

In another day and age, this area was home to thousands of Alsea Indians. With the influx of white settlers in the 1870s came a number of Germans who gave the town the name Waldport, meaning woods-port. After the town's sandy beaches had yielded a fair amount of gold dust during a short-lived gold rush, a lumber boom took hold and has remained the main industry of Waldport to this day. Dubbing itself the Salmon Fishing Capital of the World, Waldport's annual record runs of salmon and steelhead attract a swarm of sport fishermen. Nearby, Alsea Bay is also renowned for its abundance of Dungeness crab, mud clams, and razor clams. Otherwise, this quiet little coast town by the bay is proud of its "relative obscurity" which has spared it many of the afflictions faced by the more crowded tourist towns.

Sights and Attractions

Alsea Bay Bridge Historical Interpretive Center

Location: South end of the Alsea Bay Bridge, Waldport
Phone: 563–2002
Days/Hours: Daily 9–4 (summer), Wed–Sun 9–4 (rest of the year)

Operated by the Oregon State Parks Department and the Waldport Chamber of Commerce, the Interpretive Center contains many fascinating exhibits about Oregon coastal travel dating back to the early nineteenth century. A model replica of the remarkable Alsea Bay Bridge (kids will enjoy looking through a powerful scope at the real thing out the window) and photos of both the old and new bridges under construction round out the center's informative displays. In summer, the Center is base camp for the Junior Ranger Program which takes youngsters on beach and bridge walks, studies marine biology, shows informative slide and video shows, and gives each participant a certificate and button. Just ask the Center's Park Rangers for more details.

Sea Gulch

Location: 5 miles north of Waldport on Hwy 101, Seal Rock
Phone: 563–2727
Days/Hours: Daily 8–dusk (June thru Labor Day)
Cost: $3.50/adults, $2.50/seniors, $2/kids; $10/family (2 adults, 2 children)

Large, hand-carved wooden characters await your every turn as you wander the quarter mile of trails that wind through this western fantasy tourist attraction. The kids will enjoy a trek through Indian Village, Gulch City, and Boot Hill with their odd assortment of human and animal creatures. Though often striking sinister poses, the resident ruffians, peg-legged pirates, vultures, and gnomes will inspire more humor than fright. Even the legendary Bigfoot monster is somewhere to be found at Sea Gulch. Frequent demonstrations of chain-saw figure carving will fascinate the whole family. After your tour you might want to take home a few souvenirs. Six foot tall red cedar cowboys and bears ranging in size from 15 inches to eight feet are a few of the chain saw figures anxious to be planted on your porch or lawn.

Parks and Camping

Beachside State Park
Location: 4 miles south of Waldport on Hwy 101
Phone: 563–3220
Cost: Free/day use, $11–13/camping
This delightful campground (and day use area) offers 54 tent sites with fireplaces and picnic tables, 27 electrical hookups, flush toilets, hot solar showers, and many outstanding recreational attractions. Fine beachcombing, crabbing, clamming, fishing, and just plain relaxing along a half mile of broad ocean beach are what make Beachside such a popular family destination. Campers should reserve early. The park fills up quickly.

Drift Creek Wilderness
Location: 7 miles east of Waldport
A mere seven miles from the pounding Pacific surf are an incredible nine square miles of certifiable wilderness. Part of the Siuslaw National Forest, the Drift Creek Wilderness holds some of the largest remaining stands of old-growth rain forest in the Northwest. It's truly an enchanting place to explore with older children. Essentially, the terrain is mountainous, with steep, wooded ridges descending to isolated, pristine streams, canyons and meadows. There are three trails entering this paradise. The closest to Waldport is the Harris Ranch Trail which drops a quarter mile (over a two mile stretch) to a meadow adjacent to Drift Creek. For more information contact the Waldport Ranger Station at 563–3211.

Driftwood Beach State Park
Location: Off Hwy 101, 4 miles north of Waldport
As you might suspect from its name, this park is exceptionally well-littered with every imaginable size and shape of drift-

wood—a young beachcomber's dream come true. While Driftwood Park offers no camping facilities, it does provide picnic sites, drinking water, and restrooms. Its sloping terrain sits atop a squat bluff that overlooks a long beach and the ocean. Several flat, mowed lawns make great places for kids to run and play. For those wishing to hit the beach, a short, well-paved hiking trail is the best route to take.

Seal Rock State Park

Location: 4 miles north of Waldport

One of the Oregon Coast's most delightful beaches, Seal Rock State Park is especially attractive to youngsters interested in beachcombing, tidepool exploring, seal watching, and agate hunting. Its small but intriguing beach is protected by enormous cliffs and monoliths, which give it an air of seclusion. The fishing and clamming are excellent; the restless beauty of waves smashing against rocks, unsurpassed. Don't forget to bring a camera.

Annual Events

Alsea Bay Crab Festival

Location: Waldport
Date: Fourth weekend in September
Phone: 563–2133

The annual crab fest held along the streets of Old Town has been a favorite of kids of all ages since its inception in 1987. Some of the highlights include a children's parade, contests, games, prizes, food, and lots of live music. A treasure hunt sends kids and grown-ups all across the city following clues and searching for hidden markers. Of course it wouldn't be much of a crab fest without crab races, a crab ring toss, and a contest to catch the largest crab. There's plenty of crab to go around so the whole clan won't go hungry: they traditionally serve a 1,000-crab dinner, and there aren't any leftovers.

Beachcomber Days

Location: Downtown Waldport
Date: Third weekend in June
Phone: 563-2133

The whole family will find plenty to see and do at the annual Beachcomber Days festival. While the adults and teens are enjoying dances, contests, and a flea market, the kids will be occupied with a sand castle building contest, a fishing derby (children only), beach runs, and slug races. There's also a festive, traditional beer garden (adults only)—a reminder of the large number of German pioneers who settled the area in the late nineteenth century. A queen and her court preside over the Grand Parade, bringing a touch of old world royalty down Main Street.

YACHATS

Yachats ("ya-hots") is a gem of a resort town nestled at the base of coastal hills. Its 500 residents have built their homes and cottages on these gentle slopes and kept commercial development to a minimum. Vacationers have long sensed that Yachats is a place to come enjoy a sleepy tranquility unknown at most of the "action" spots along the coast. Rocky shores, fine sandy beaches, small coves, great eateries and lodging, and the nearby Yachats River beckon to visitors in search of a "quality" experience. The April through October smelt season attracts anglers from all over the West in pursuit of these sardine-like fish which come to shore to spawn. Quiet, demure Yachats blows off a bit of steam in celebration of the annual smelt run with the Smelt Fry in July.

Sights and Attractions

Cape Perpetua Visitor Center

Location: 3 miles south of Yachats off Hwy 101
Phone: 547–3289
Days/Hours: Daily 10–5

This popular "attraction" is visited by over 60,000 travellers each year. No wonder. The views alone are spectacular from this highest point on the Oregon Coast. On a clear day, you can almost see forever. The un-aided eye can take in 40 miles out to sea, and 75 miles up and down the coast. The Center's movies, short videos, and exhibits will introduce young and old alike to such topics as coastal tides and weather, ocean-going ships, whale migration, and archaeology. It's a presentation that even young children will find fascinating. After touring the Center, be sure to visit the marine Garden Reserve Tidepools.

Cape Perpetua offers many fine viewpoints for catching sight of gray whales migrating southward along the coast in January and February and northward throughout the spring months. Several trails lead out from the center (some easy, others moderate to difficult) going deep into old growth forest or under the highway to the beach. A free guide to these hiking trails is available at the Center. For a real thrill, take the self-guided auto tour which turns off from the road above the Center. On your ascent to the top of Cape Perpetua you'll twist and turn along a steep, windy, narrow road (paved, of course) through forested hills. The roller coaster covers about 18 miles and returns you to Highway 101. The descent is truly breath-taking. Through the giant trees you'll catch spectacular glimpses of the blue Pacific far below. It's the kind of drive that the child in us all loves to take. Which makes it surprising that most visitors don't make this exhilarating trip up the cape.

Devil's Churn

Location: Just north of the junction of Cape Perpetua Rd. & Hwy 101

Devil's Churn provides a close up look at the awesome power

of the surf as the sea attacks the oceanside cliffs. As the tides thunder and crash against the rocky walls, great gobs of foam, much like whipped cream, are tossed in every direction. Your children will love all the commotion—and so will you. Parking and restrooms are provided, along with walkways and paths that lead down to a viewing area of the churning activity. Watch out for dangerous "sneaker waves" and definitely hold on to younger children if you decide to venture beyond the observation point for a closer look at all the action. Devil's Churn is an excellent spot for photographers.

Gwynn Creek Trail
Location: About 3.5 miles south of Yachats
A totally different coastal experience awaits hikers on the Gwynn Creek Trail. This out-of-the-ordinary trek is a trip back in time. At first the route follows a portion of the Oregon Coast Trail, itself once a main wagon road for pioneer travellers between Florence and Waldport. After about a mile, the Oregon Coast Trail crosses the Gwynn Creek Trail, which climbs up a canyon through magnificent, towering stands of old-growth fir and spruce. In places the forest is so densely packed that it seems as if night has suddenly descended. It's a little eerie. Stop and share a spooky story. Able hikers can continue this moderately difficult walk for about 6.5 miles, looping back to the Cape Perpetua Visitor Center. Maps and trail directions are available at the Cape Perpetua Visitor Center.

Little Log Church Museum
Location: Third & Pontiac Sts., Yachats
Phone: 547–3530
Days/Hours: Daily 10–4
Cost: Free
This log church was built during the great Depression by local volunteers to serve as a community place of worship for all denominations. In the late '60s it was donated to the historical society as a museum. It now features a collection of Indian artifacts and household items used by the pioneers, such as clothing, tools, furniture, kitchen items, and even a working

pump organ. These displays provide a great opportunity for parents to share a bit of the past with their children. There's also a fascinating assemblage of photos along one wall documenting the area's major road and highway construction activities which commenced in the early 1900s. The Little Log Church by the sea is a favorite site for weddings. Check with the Chamber of Commerce at 547-3530 for more information.

Strawberry Hill

Location: 3.5 miles south of Yachats off Hwy 101

Strawberry Hill, carpeted in the spring with the blossoms of the low growing wild coastal strawberry, is a great spot to explore tidepools and observe harbor seals. The seals spend their days fishing the cold waters of the Pacific, then relaxing on the rocky bluffs just 25 yards offshore. They loll about, especially at low tide, permitting a close look and a nice picture—although if you're heading out with kids in tow, be careful since the rocks can be quite slippery. Low tide is also the best time to check out some of the most interesting tidepools on the entire coast. Young explorers will be intrigued by the sea anemones, kelp, seaweed, spiny sea urchins, turban snails, and hermit crabs that teem in these tidepools. Birdlife abounds at Strawberry Hill. Cormorants, gulls, pelicans, and oyster catchers can all be seen plying their trades. Interestingly, most travellers on Highway 101 drive right past the inconspicuous turnoff sign without guessing what adventures lie here. The parking area is hidden from highway view by a mound, which probably accounts for all the non-stoppers. Since it's uncrowded, Strawberry Hill an ideal place to spend "quality" time.

Yachats River Beach

Location: South of the Yachats River Bridge

Psst. This is one of those secret places known to but a few. Until now, of course. When local residents have young children visiting, they usually take them down to play on the sandy beach at the entrance to the Yachats River. At low tide the water is shallow with virtually no waves present. The children get to frolic in the sand and water while the adults enjoy the sight. You can get to this beach from the Yachats Ocean Wayside, a short distance south of the river bridge.

Parks and Camping

Neptune State Park
Location: 3 miles south of Yachats off Hwy 101
This scenic park has it all. A beautiful, though small, sandy beach, about two miles of rugged, rocky ocean front, picnic tables, restroom facilities, and only a scattering of people. Young agile climbers will have an easy time accessing the many tidepools in the rocks at the south end of the beach. With few visitors, these rocks offer plenty of solitary spots from which to admire the beauty of the surrounding sights and enjoy the sounds of the swirling sea.

Smelt Sands Wayside
Location: North end of Yachats
Except for several weeks in July when the seasonal smelt run draws crowds, this beach is an ideal family getaway. Grown ups can savor the solitude while marveling at the waves that slam against the rocky shoreline. Young beachcombers love this tiny, sandless beach covered with a beautiful carpet of marble-sized gravel and shiny agate chips. To reach Smelt Sands Wayside, go west at the state parks sign at the north end of Yachats and take the left fork of the gravel entrance road.

Annual Events

Arts and Crafts Fair
Location: The Commons (formerly Yachats School)
Date: Third weekend in March
Phone: 547–3530
A pleasant springtime weekend can be spent enjoying the many colorful sights and sounds of the Yachats Arts and Crafts

Fair. Artists and craftspeople offer a wide variety of hand-made items of clay, wood, leather, and fabric, while the food purveyors flood the celebration with scents of fresh baked goods, seafoods, and of course, the "best homemade chili this side of Texas."

Yachats Kite Festival

Location: On the beach at the Yachats River Bridge
Date: First Saturday in October
Phone: 547–3530

For nearly twenty years, kite flyers (and lots of spectators) have flocked to this beach to take part in the annual kite festival. It's a wide-open event with no rules as to kite size, shape, or type. Kids of all ages, be they serious or amateur flyers, will have a great time as they take to the air with their motley group of high-flying kites. Everything from the simplest homemade variety to the best store-bought models is welcome to share the air space high over the ocean and compete for prizes that have been donated by Yachats merchants. A kite-flying contest works up a hearty appetite, which the food vendors who offer chili, franks, and homemade pastries, will happily satisfy.

10

FLORENCE

Legend has it that the town was named after a French sailing vessel that foundered offshore. A piece of the shipwreck floated ashore bearing the name "Florence" and the tiny new metropolis had a name. Of course, there are some who disagree. Town curmudgeons love to pooh-pooh the myth by pointing out that Florence was likely named after a state senator who lived here before the Civil War. Visitors are free to make their own decisions.

Modern Florence, located mid-way along Oregon's coastal route, has seen an influx of thousands of retirees in recent years. Its proximity to culture and shopping in Eugene (an hour away), a mild climate, and a moderate cost of living all help explain the senior rush to Florence. Vacationers are drawn by the town's access to the National Dunes Recreation Area, by its fine river and ocean fishing, crabbing, and clamming, and by its picturesque shops and eateries in historic Old Town.

Sights and Attractions

Blue Max Scenic Flights

Location: 2001 Airport Way, Florence Municipal Airport
Phone: 997–8069
Days/Hours: Daily 10–6
Cost: $50 for up to 3 people

For a truly unforgettable perspective of the blue Pacific, coastal hills and forests, climb aboard the Blue Max flying machine. The air tour lasts about a half-hour and includes passes over hidden lakes and rivers. Up to three sightseers can squeeze aboard each flight. Reservations are accepted, but not required. Though you won't be needing your sea legs that high over the water, you are advised to bring your cameras. The photo opportunities are spectacular.

C & M Stables

Location: 90241 Hwy 101 North, 8 miles north of Florence
Phone: 997–7540
Days/Hours: Daily 8 am–11 pm (summer), Wed–Sun 10 am–
  4 pm (winter)
Cost: $15/hr. per person

Ever imagine a family horseback ride on the beach—especially at sunset as the sun's red glow lingers on the horizon? Your children will love it. C & M Stables welcomes riders of all skill levels. Their experienced wranglers personally assign each rider a saddle and a horse that's just right. The beach ride starts out from the stables and winds down a lush, fragrant forest trail passing through some of the most scenic dunes on the Oregon coast. A ride on the beach and through the surf is truly an experience you won't soon forget.

Carter Dunes Trail

Location: Off Hwy 101, 8.5 miles south of Florence

This trail is ideal for children to hike since it's a short trek of only .25 miles from its trailhead in Carter Lake Campground into the dunes. The hike itself through dense forest is a delight, but the real fun for young adventurers starts as the trail ends in the dunes. Since there's no developed trail in this portion of the dunes, hikers have the freedom to explore wherever they like as they march toward the sea. If you visit this portion of the dunes from winter through early summer, large areas of standing water may be encountered. These marshy areas abound in wildlife, making great places to share splendid nature views with the kids. Another feature of the dunes here: quiet and solitude. Motorized vehicles are banned, and the silence can be golden.

Dolly Wares Doll Museum

Location: 2 miles north of Florence on Hwy 101 at 36th St.
Phone: 997–3391
Days/Hours: Tues–Sun 10–5
Cost: $3.50/adults, $2/ages 5–12
Dolls, dolls, and more dolls (nearly 3,000 to be exact) make up a collection that's been growing for half a century. This museum will fascinate youngsters and oldsters alike with its impressive variety of dolls and original costumes. The oldest, a four inch crude clay doll, dates to pre-Columbian times. There are wooden dolls made in the 1600s. Dolls of all kinds, shapes, and sizes fill every nook and cranny. The largest is over six feet tall while the smallest could fit comfortably in the palm of your hand. Plastic dolls, metal dolls, china dolls, wax dolls, papier-mâché dolls—whatever the material, you'll probably find a doll made of it here.

Fly Fishing Museum

Location: 280 Nopal St., Florence
Phone: 997–6102
Days/Hours: Daily 10–5
Cost: $2.50/adults, free/under 16
This is probably the finest collection of fishing flies to be found anywhere in the western United States. This second story museum, just a few blocks from the Old Town waterfront, has accumulated flies (some from the early 1800s) from all over the

world. It's an unusual, but fascinating collection that most youngsters, especially those who fish, will enjoy. Angling scenes and wood sculptures round out the collection.

Heceta Head Lighthouse

Location: Devil's Elbow State Park; on Hwy 101, 12 miles north of Florence

Days/Hours: Daily 9–dusk

Standing majestically over 200 feet above the pounding surf, Heceta Head Lighthouse makes up part of the quintessential beauty of the Oregon Coast. The brilliant white tower, with its roof of red tiles, perches precariously on a ledge high above the sea. The lighthouse, built a century ago, is Oregon's most powerful beacon—and probably America's most photographed lighthouse. It's not unusual when the fog rolls in, to imagine something's amiss here. Look out over the cliffs. It was over a hundred years ago that the wife of the first lighthouse keeper fell to her death from these cliffs. Stories have stubbornly persisted that the lighthouse is haunted. Some have claimed to have seen a ghostly figure moving about in the mist. It's a story that imaginative youngsters thrill to hear. A short hike to the beach reveals some great picnicking spots and beachcombing opportunities, though nothing supernatural.

Indian Forest

Location: 88493 Hwy 101 North, Florence

Phone: 997–3677

Days/Hours: Daily 8–8 (June thru Aug), 10–4 (May, Sept & October)

Cost: $4/adults, $3/ages 12–18, $2/ages 5–11, free/under 5 years

At the giant, colored totem pole four miles north of Florence, turn in and leave the 20th century behind. An adventure awaits the whole family along a winding foot path that leads through a coastal forest of huckleberries and rhododenrons to full-sized authentic recreations of Native American dwellings. Wigwams, tepees, and hogans are all on display here. Don't be startled to come face to face with real deer and buffalo that roam the grounds. The Indian Trading Post gift shop offers a wide selection of handmade native-American arts and crafts: jewelry, pottery, dolls, toys, rugs, baskets, and moccasins.

Old Town
Location: Bay St., Florence

Florence's historic business center is home to a cluster of restaurants and specialty shops offering a variety of food, clothing, gifts, antiques, crafts, art, and other first-rate items— all housed in restored historic buildings. Children will love such incredible edibles as homemade ice creams and pastries. With over 60 shops to explore and a scenic location along the mouth of the Siuslaw River to boot, Old Town is a "must" in any Oregon Coast visitor's travel plans.

Oregon Dunes Overlook
Location: Between Florence and Reedsport on Hwy 101

Many travellers zipping by on Highway 101 used to fail to notice the dunes because the trees pretty well obscure them from traffic. What was needed was an overlook and that's just what the Forest Service came up with. Youngsters will find the interpretive signs here an excellent introduction to the various dune forms. Forest Service interpreters are available from 10 a.m. to 3 p.m. to answer any questions. Children will especially enjoy climbing each of the four levels of enclosed viewing platforms that are connected by walkways. The views of the dunes, forested "islands," and the sea are extraordinary from these platforms. A short trail (about a quarter mile) leads from the overlook to the dunes. Then it's less than a mile through sand and wetlands to the ocean.

Sand Dune Vehicle Rentals/Tours

*See introduction to "Sand Dune Vehicle Rentals/
Tours" in Chapter 12.*

Sand Dunes Frontier

Location: 83960 Hwy 101, 4 miles south of Florence
Phone: 997–3544
Days/Hours: Daily 9–dusk (March thru October)
Cost: Dune bus tours: $6/adults, $3/under 10; minicars:
$35/hr.

Dune bus tours run about thirty minutes long. Hourly
rates on ATV minicar rentals go down the longer the
rental period. Other attractions include an 18-hole miniature golf course, a stocked fish pond, and a game arcade.

Sandland Adventures, Inc.

Location: Hwy 101 at 10th St., Florence
Phone: 997–8087
Days/Hours: Daily 9–dusk (weather permitting)
Cost: Dune buggies: $30/hr; 4-wheelers: $35/hr; dune
buggy tours: $15/person

Offers a variety of "you drive" and "we drive" packages,
with rates reduced for longer term rentals. Reservations
recommended, but walk-ins welcomed, too.

Seahorse Stagecoach

Location: 270 Hwy 101, Florence
Phone: 964–3174
Days/Hours: Sat & Sun 10–4
Cost: $5/adults, $4/seniors, $3/under 14

Kids love climbing aboard the seahorse stagecoach to take an
enchanting three mile trip back in time. The coach holds up to
16 people and boasts a "high-tech" heating system composed

of an on-board wood-burning stove and blankets. The trip along the packed, wet sand lasts about an hour, often providing a look at harbor seals and sea lions frolicking in the nearby surf. For young riders, a trip aboard this quaint sea coach provides a wonderful opportunity to experience how Oregonians actually travelled along the coast in the early part of this century. Round trip coach rides run every weekend of the year between Florence's north jetty and the Driftwood Shores Hotel—except during storms. Pick up your ride either at the jetty (take Highway 101 to 35th St., then west to Rhododendron Dr., go north and follow signs to jetty) or at the Driftwood Shores Hotel located at 88416 First Avenue in Florence.

Sea Lion Caves
Location: 91560 Hwy 101, 10 miles north of Florence
Phone: 547-3111
Days/Hours: Daily 9–7 (summer), 9–4 (winter)
Cost: $5/adults, $3/ages 6–15, free/5 years and under
As you descend over 200 feet by elevator into one of the world's largest sea caves, you'll be stunned by what you see and hear. A 12-story building surrounded by a football field could easily be accommodated within this massive wave-carved grotto. Hundreds of huge sea lions, some weighing up to a ton apiece, gather on the rocks in this natural amphitheater to bark, roar, and wheeze at the top of their lungs.While the grownups squirm and find all this cacophony a bit much, the children clearly love it.

Strange as it may seem, you enter Sea Lion Caves through the gift shop on Highway 101. A steep downhill walk to the elevator reveals close-up, stunning views of coastal cliffs and the birds that nest there. In fall and winter the sea lions occupy the cave, while the rest of the year they're out on the nearby rocky ledges. Whatever the season, the sight of these giant sea mammals frolicking in their natural habitat should not be missed—despite a cave-stench that will leave quite a lingering impression.

Siltcoos Lake Trail

Location: Off Hwy 101, 8 miles of Florence

Adults and kids alike will be delighted by the many natural attractions found along the Siltcoos Lake Trail. Snaking through a canopy of dense, second growth forest, the trail passes marshes, freshwater springs, giant cedar snags, and a scattering of huge stumps left over from the early days of timbering. It's a little eerie in places, but fun. About half way to the lake the trail divides, making a loop option for returning to the trailhead. As you get closer to the lake you'll notice an increasing abundance of wildlife. Kids will love seeing the many birds and small mammals in their natural habitat. Hearts young and old usually quicken at the occasional sighting of a deer or black bear rushing off through the dense underbrush.

Siuslaw Pioneer Museum

Location: 85294 Hwy 101 South, Florence
Phone: 997–7884
Days/Hours: Tues-Sun 10–4 (closed month of December)
Cost: Free

Housed in a former church, this museum is a fine place for children to learn all about the early history of Florence. They'll see many interesting exhibits, including pioneer clothing, tools, and pictures as well as a complete pioneer kitchen (how could any kitchen without microwaves, cuisinarts, and toasters be complete?). A display of Indian artifacts accompanies storyboards which tell the sad story of how the Siuslaw tribe was hoodwinked by the U.S. Government into selling Indian lands without compensation.

Westward Ho Sternwheeler Cruises

Location: Odom's Landing in Tiernan, between Florence and Mapleton
Phone: 268–4017
Days/Hours: Call for schedule (May thru October)
Cost: $10/person

As in days of yore, sternwheel paddle boat travel has returned to Oregon's waterways. Passengers can cruise the Suislaw

River aboard an exact scale replica of the sternwheelers that plied these waters a century and a half ago. The 65-foot Westward Ho, with a 50 passenger capacity, offers morning cruises to Mapleton (about 15 miles east of Florence) and afternoon cruises into Old Town Florence. Throughout the cruise, onboard interpreters recount the historical events that occurred on the river. Of special interest to children is the diversity of wildlife observable from on deck.

Parks and Camping

Alder Dune Campground
Location: On Hwy 101, 7 miles north of Florence
Phone: (800) 283–CAMP (for reservations)
Cost: $8/camping (June thru September)
Alder Dune features 39 lake view campsites that are nicely separated from one another by trees and dense brush. Besides such usual amenities as tree-shaded sites, fireplaces, water, and flush toilets, the park is home to beautiful, but tiny Alder Lake. Although the lake is a bit cramped for boating and water skiing, there's an abundance of other recreational opportunities available, including swimming, fishing, canoeing, and lakeside picnicking. Several trails allow for short hikes around the lake, or longer ones across sand dunes and to the beach. With a keen eye for spotting recreational opportunities missed by their parents, children are quick to observe that several dunes slope into the lake. In a jiffy they're experts at downhill dune sliding and lake kerplunking.

Darlingtonia Botanical Wayside
Location: Mercer Lake Rd., off Hwy 101; 4 miles north of Florence
Days/Hours: Daily, 9–dusk
Darlingtonia Wayside, a state botanical preserve, is home to the carnivorous Darlingtonia plants. Also known as "cobra lilies," these bug-eating plants trap and devour insects. Raised wooden walkways safely guide visitors above spooky bogs and

through dense growths of cobra lilies resembling the snakes poised to strike. Display boards illustrate the whole gory process and if you still feel like eating afterwards there are picnic tables and restrooms nearby. The half-mile nature hike is most interesting from April to June when the cobra lilies are blooming.

Devil's Elbow State Park

Location: 13 miles north of Florence on Hwy 101
Visitors to Devil's Elbow will find an inviting, cozy little cove with nearby amenities (restrooms, picnic tables, drinking water) and fine ocean vistas. Young rockhounds will love it here as the receding tides can uncover some fine "collectibles." Take the nearby trail up to Heceta Head Lighthouse. It's an easy walk up and the exceptional views on the way back afford some outstanding photographic opportunities.

Driftwood II Campground

Location: 1.25 miles off Hwy 101, 10 miles south of Florence
Cost: $6/camping
In addition to the usual amenities, this popular family campground of over 90 tent-trailer sites provides such child-pleasers as direct access to the sand dunes and several hiking trails that wind through thick coastal forest en route to Siltcoos Lake.

Florence City Parks

Miller Park

Location: 18th St. West, off Hwy 101, Florence
This large, nicely-landscaped 20 acre park features several ball fields, a jogging path, playground equipment, a refreshment stand, and restrooms. It's truly a lovely place for a family outing.

Munsel Creek Greenway Park

Location: Willow at 24th St., Florence
Amenities include a stream and wooded area, sand dunes,

a summer lake, rock-strewn pathways, and restrooms. This 18 acre park is ideally suited for studying local wildlife in its natural habitat. It's also a fine place for children, as the water and the woods provide imaginative play areas.

Munsel Road Park

Location: Munsel Lake Rd., Florence

Munsel Park is a nice neighborhood park that's ideal for small children. The play area and playground equipment are fenced in, keeping little ones from wandering off while the grownups are taking a breather. A well-maintained basketball court can also be found here.

Pepperoaks Park

Location: 34th Place, Florence

Visitors to this small, cozy, neighborhood park will find a basketball court, picnic tables, and playground equipment.

Pocket Park

Location: 18th St., Florence

Pocket Park, another of Florence's small neighborhood parks, features a basketball court, an open sand area, and rugged playground equipment for both big and little kids.

Rolling Dunes Park

Location: 35th St. at Siano Loop, Florence

Located near scenic sand dunes, the park contains two tennis courts, a horseshoe pit, sheltered picnic tables and restrooms. It's rarely crowded and makes a good place to stop for a picnic if you're travelling.

Singing Pines Park

Location: Airport Rd. at 15th St., Florence

This heavily wooded seven acre park features sturdy play

equipment and several paths that loop through a dense pine forest. Kids will find lots of woods to explore in this urban wilderness park.

Lagoon Campground
Location: .75 miles off Hwy 101, 10 miles south of Florence
Cost: $6/camping (May thru October)
Forty tent-trailer campsites can be found at Lagoon, along with picnic tables, water, and fireplaces. In summer, a multitude of family oriented weekend programs are held at the campground amphitheater. Several popular trails attract hikers to the area. Across the road lies easy access to the Siltcoos River Fisherman's Trail. Closer at hand, the River of No Return Nature Trail rings the campground. It's a favorite with children, not only because it sounds sinister, but because of the abundance of wildlife found along the trail. Lagoon Campground has no trailer hookups or boat launching ramp, although use of car-top boats is allowed.

Honeyman State Park
Location: 84505 Hwy 101, 3 miles south of Florence
Phone: 997–3851
Cost: Free/day use, $9–13/camping
This gem of a recreation area located several miles south of Florence is adjacent to a sparkling freshwater swimming lake that's bordered by stark-white sand dunes. With picnic tables well-spaced along the shore, and clean, soft sand, Honeyman is a honey of an eating and sunbathing spot. An abundance of dunes, some over 250 feet high, create a vast, inviting playground. Nearby Lake Woahink, accessible by road and trail, offers such popular pastimes as waterskiing, boating, and fishing. It also has a sentional swimming hole that kids will love. Stroll a bit farther, and you'll arrive at the ocean and beaches that seem to go on forever. With nearly 400 campsites, well maintained facilities, lots of scenic hiking trails, and nearby dune buggy rental companies, Honeyman State Park happens to be one of the West's best-kept campground secrets.

Oregon Dunes National Recreation Area

Location: Along the coast between Florence & Coos Bay

Florence is the gateway to one of the world's largest sand piles. Stretching along the coast for over forty miles (and between two to four miles wide) the Dunes National Recreation Area is a remarkable landscape of awesome sand dunes, small patches of pine forests, lakes, and sandy beaches. Hiking, horseback riding, dune buggying, boating, water skiing, fishing, swimming, camping, and beachcombing are many of the popular ways to explore and enjoy this fantastic recreation area. Ironically, even with all these things to do, many tourists on Highway 101 simply drive by because the dunes are pretty well obscured from highway view by strips of forest.

Some things to keep in mind when visiting the dunes: Although the Dunes National Recreation Area is a sensational family recreation area, it holds some serious hazards. Visitors, and most certainly those with children, need to be aware. The sand, especially near popular areas, can contain broken glass and other harmful debris covered by blowing and shifting sand. Getting lost in the dunes can be very easy when you consider that blowing sand can wipe out footprints and reduce visibility. When the fog races in and everything becomes a blur, panic can set in, especially as the sun sinks toward the horizon.

To get more from your visit to this giant vacationland, refer to the following listings in this book: Oregon Dunes Visitor Center (Reedsport), Honeyman State Park (Florence), C & M Stables (Florence), Sand Dunes Frontier (Florence), and the Oregon Dunes Overlook (Florence).

Sutton Campground

Location: Hwy 101, 6 miles north of Florence
Phone: 268–4473
Cost: $8/camping

The campground's 80 grassy sites are situated just a short 15 minute hike from ocean beaches, dunes, and Sutton Lake. Amenities include picnic tables, fireplaces, water, flush toilets, and swimming and fishing at Sutton Creek—located a mere stone's throw from the campground. The horseshoe pit is always a popular family hangout here. A well-marked, easy-to-hike trail leads to the Darlingtonia Wayside, where incredible bug-eating plants can be seen in action. For imaginative youngsters, the summer campfire talks and activities held in the campground amphitheater are pure magic.

Washburne Memorial State Park

Location: 14 miles north of Florence on Hwy 101

This long stretch of clean, sandy beach seems pretty much overlooked by the crowds that choose to descend instead on Devil's Elbow State Park, a few miles to the south. Which means, of course, that lonely, windswept Washburne makes a great place for kite flying or just running up and down the beach. Young beachcombers and tidepoolers will enjoy the fine offerings here. If you really want to get away from it all, try hiking down to the south end of Washburne where the crowd will usually consist of only you and your companions. Start your trek at the park's picnic area and head south over a small stream or two. If you prefer to arrive with dry feet, drive 1.2 miles south of the Washburne parking lot entrance on Highway 101. On the east side of the highway you'll see a paved pull-off. Park, then cross the highway and follow the trail to the beach below.

Waxmyrtle Campground

Location: .75 miles west of Hwy 101, 10 miles south of Florence

Cost: $6/camping

Waxmyrtle provides 56 tent-trailer campsites, along with picnic tables, fireplaces, drinking water, toilets, but no hookups. Its proximity to sand dunes, freshwater lakes, and the ocean makes it an attractive campground for families with youngsters interested in fishing, hiking, and swimming. Although there are no boat ramps at Waxmyrtle, car-top boats are allowed.

Annual Events

Oregon Dunes Mushers Mail Run

Date: Second weekend in March
Phone: 997–3128
An annual event since 1977, the Mushers Mail Run has been pitting dog sledders from the western United States and Canada against each other in a grueling test of endurance across miles of high sand dunes and forest trails. Special four-wheel sleds are raced from the start at North Bend to the finish line on the dunes west of Florence. It's an action-packed, fun-filled event the entire family will enjoy watching. The dogs and their mushers can best be seen in action on the last day of the run from the Dunes Overlook (on Highway 101 between Florence and Reedsport). All the teams come together after the race for a grand parade in Florence's Old Town, where thousands line the route to salute the mushers and participate in the end-of-the-run festivities. Young souvenir hounds will be delighted to buy a commemorative envelope, carried and autographed by the driver of each racing team, and hand cancelled at Post Offices in North Bend and Florence.

Rhododendron Festival

Date: Third weekend in May
Phone: 997–3128
For one weekend, Florence explodes with color and pageantry at the annual rhododendron festival. There's so much here for kids to see and do, you'd think the event was custom made especially for them, but it's truly an all-ages weekend. Tens of thousands of visitors come help Florence celebrate by participating in parades, sailboard races, slug races, the Rhody Run, sports tournaments, the carnival, arts and crafts exhibits, the queen's coronation, and more. The Grand Floral Parade is not to be missed, with its abundance of flower-studded floats, horses, and of course—lots of clowns. Adding to the mirth and merriment are roving food and craft vendors selling their wares on the streets. The Rhododendron Festival is in its 85th year and continues a very long tradition of bringing good old-fashioned fun and excitement to thousands.

11

REEDSPORT

Although originally built on marshland, modern Reedsport no longer has to cope with the constant flooding that came with the high tides. A dike was built in the early 1960s, after a devastating flood, to protect the lower part of town. Long before the dike, however, early Reedsporters put their buildings and walkways on stilts, up to eight feet above the marshy ground. No doubt in response to many a citizen dropping off the sidewalks, clay was taken from nearby hills and used to fill in the ground.

Reedsport, bounded by rivers, lakes, and the ocean, is a near-perfect setting for outdoor adventuring. Nearby Salmon Harbor Marina at Winchester Bay is one of Oregon's finest sport-fishing marinas. Striped bass, Chinook and silver salmon, and steelhead trout lure anglers in the waters around Reedsport. Many of the town's 5,000 residents operate businesses along Highway 101 feeding, lodging, and otherwise catering to the needs of travellers, dune hikers, and fishermen.

Sights and Attractions

Dean Creek Interpretive Center

Location: 3 miles east of Reedsport on Hwy 38

This recently constructed center, located in the Dean Creek Elk Viewing Area, affords spectacular observations of a herd of more than 100 wild and majestic Roosevelt Elk which makes its home in this nature preserve. Male elk can weigh over 700 pounds and support a massive "hat rack." Most of the time the elk are clearly visible from Highway 38, usually munching and roaming about the meadow. The interpretive center affords a safe look at the animals and is preferable by far to "rubber-necking" on the highway. Colorful display panels feature (what else?) Roosevelt Elk. It's an interesting, educational stop.

Hero

Location: Off Hwy 38, left on 2nd St., Reedsport
Phone: 271–2605 or (800) 247–2155
Days/ Hours: Daily 10–4 (summer), by request (winter)
Cost: $3/person, $10/family

Kids love bounding across the gangplank to board the Hero, the world-famous ship that explored the vast frozen Antarctic wasteland. Visitors can tour this 300 ton vessel and see how its unique design permitted its crew of 12, plus seven scientists, to eat, sleep, and perform a multitude of scientific experiments for several months at a time. Explorers of all ages will have fun inspecting the Hero's two laboratories which were equipped for physical oceanography, bio-acoustic studies, on-shore geology, and biological investigations. Its hull was specially designed to withstand the coldest conditions imaginable. Although now retired, the vessel is just as it was when it returned from its last Antarctic voyage, with dishes, bedding, maps, and equipment left where the crew last put them.

Oregon Dunes Visitor Center

Location: 855 Hwy Ave., at intersection of Hwy 101 and 38, Reedsport
Phone: 271–3611
Days/Hours: Mon–Fri 8–4:30, Sat & Sun 10–5:30
The best way to start your visit to the Oregon Dunes National Recreation Area is to first drop in at the visitor center. There you'll find a friendly, helpful staff willing to answer all questions. They offer brochures at no charge that cover a range of topics from whale watching to plant identification. Soon-to-be dune adventurers will be chomping at the bit to get out on the sand after watching a short, but fascinating film on the sand dunes. The center also provides a wealth of summer activities and interpretive programs. You can choose from daily two-hour guided nature walks, monthly full-day guided hikes (these can get quite strenuous!), monthly two-hour guided "Dunebusters" (perfect outing for children), and weekend campfire programs. The focus of all these fun-filled activities is on the wide variety of wildlife, plant life, and geological phenomena found at the dunes. Interpretive programs run from Memorial Day through Labor Day.

Sand Dune Vehicle Rentals/Tours

See introduction to "Sand Dune Vehicle Rentals/ Tours" in Chapter 12.

Dunes Odyssey Rentals

Location: On Hwy 101, Winchester Bay
Phone: 271–4011
Days/Hours: Daily 8–dusk (closed Wednesdays in winter)
Cost: Dune buggies & 4-wheelers: $30/hr.
All vehicles are priced the same, with additional rental hours reduced by $5 per hour.

Dune Quad Runners

Location: 9th & Salmon, Winchester Bay
Phone: 271-3443
Days/Hours: Daily 9-dusk
Cost: Dune buggies: from $25/hr.; 4-wheelers: from $35/hr.

Dune Quad Runners offers one of the largest selections of machines on the entire Oregon Coast. Rates decrease for each additional rental hour, with special half-day and day rates available.

Tahkenitch Lake

Location: On Hwy 101, 7 miles north of Reedsport

Because of its irregular shape (the Indian word Tahkenitch means "many arms"), this lake of 1,600 acres actually has over 100 miles of shoreline offering endless beaches for families to explore. Visitors come from afar to fish, boat, and view the area's wildlife. A boat ramp and dock make for easy access out to this lake and its' abundant salmon, bass, perch, and trout. Forty species of birds, including a few species of mammals and amphibians, also reside at Tahkenitch Lake and are regularly observed.

Threemile Lake and Trail

Location: Off Hwy 101, 7 miles north of Reedsport

This easy to moderate three mile trail starts out at a junction about .25 miles south of the trailhead at Tahkenitch Lake. It proceeds west through a conifer forest that imaginative youngsters will find enchanting. Continuing past small freshwater lakes and marshes, up hills that unfold sweeping views of dunes and sea, the trail finally reaches its final destination: Threemile Lake. Besides a large fish population of perch and trout, the lake area is home to a considerable variety of wildlife. Black bears, coyotes, deer, mink, beavers, and otters are among the animals that have been observed here. Camping is permitted, although there are no backcountry facilities. However, the trail is ideally suited for backpack campers since many open, mossy site possibilities exist along the trek to Threemile Lake.

Umpqua River Lighthouse

Location: 5 miles south of Reedsport, off Hwy 101 at Winchester Bay
Phone: 271-4118
Days/Hours: Museum, Wed-Sat 10-5, Sun 1-5 (May-September 30)

Since 1894, this impressive lighthouse has been guiding ships along the Oregon coast and into the mouth of the Umpqua River. Measuring 67 feet in height and standing 165 feet above the pounding surf, the Umpqua Lighthouse casts a beam seen 20 miles out at sea. It is one of the few lighthouses that uses the original lenses—made in Paris a century ago. The Lighthouse Museum, at the base of the tower, is a former United States Coast Guard bachelor quarters later used to house lighthouse keepers. Pictures of sailing schooners and stern-wheel river steamers crowd the walls. The museum also documents the construction of Fort Umpqua, which was designed to protect settlers and lighthouse workers from unfriendly Indians. Kids and adults will find the Coast Guard lifesaving exhibits and rescue craft on display here fascinating. Near the lighthouse, a whale watching platform provides a safe and convenient place to view California gray whales as they migrate southward along the coast in January and February and return again in the opposite direction from March through May.

Winchester Bay

Location: 4 miles southwest of Reedsport, off Hwy 101

The real gem in Winchester Bay is Salmon Harbor—the largest recreational salmon port on the entire Oregon coast. An abundance of charter boats offer daily ocean fishing excursions and provide all the necessary equipment. If you've brought along your own craft, you'll find launching and moorage available at this excellent full-service marina. For those wishing to stay closer to land, a nearby pier juts out into the Umpqua River. Crabbing and fishing are both popular and rewarding pastimes from the pier. The bay area also teems with other recreational opportunities. Nearby Salmon Harbor Basin County Park offers playground facilities, picnicking, fishing, and boat launching. Windy Cove Park has all these amenities plus lots of tent sites and hookups. Although the once sleepy village of Winchester Bay has blossomed into a recreational powerhouse, the town still has that pleasant, unassuming feel to it.

Parks and Camping

Carter Lake Campground
Location: On Hwy 101, 11 miles north of Reedsport
Cost: $6/night (May thru October)
The campground's 22 paved sites, with such amenities as picnic tables, water, flush toilets, and fireplaces, are set out among a pine forest filled with songbirds, black-tailed deer, and Pacific treefrogs that occasionally meander or hop by. Carter Lake, 40-feet deep and covering 28 acres, attracts fishermen with its stock of trout and bass. A boat ramp is available.

North Eel Campground
Location: Off Hwy 101, 9 miles south of Reedsport
Phone: 271–4639
Cost: $6/night
Facilities include 53 tent-trailer sites with toilets, water, and fireplaces, but no trailer hook-ups. The two mile west trail runs through a wide, vast expanse of open sand to the sea. Nearby Eel Creek is easily accessible from the campground. Slide shows are held on summer weekends at the campground amphitheater.

Tahkenitch Campground
Location: Off Hwy 101, 7 miles north of Reedsport
Cost: $6/night
Campers can expect to find 36 tent-trailer sites with picnic tables, fireplaces, water, and toilets, although no hook ups are available. Several hundred varieties of birds and 80 species of

mammals may be observed in the nearby marshes. The campground is also the trailhead for the Tahkenitch Trail which makes a beeline into the dunes. It's about .75 miles to the open sand, then about an additional mile to the beach. Before reaching its destination, the trail heads through lush coastal evergreens, arriving at a scenic dunes viewpoint seemingly designed just for camera buffs.

Umpqua Lighthouse State Park

Location: .5 miles off Hwy 101, 6 miles south of Reedsport
Phone: 271–4118
Cost: Free/day use, $11–13/camping (April thru October)
Umpqua State Park offers campers 42 tent sites and 22 full hookup sites; day users will find picnic areas, water, and restrooms. Located in forested, hilly terrain, the park overlooks a small, sparkling fresh-water lake that's a good swimming hole for children. The beach here is ideal for beachcombing, strolling, or just plain basking in the sun. The area is rich in recreational opportunities. The nearby jetty at the mouth of Winchester Bay is a popular fishing spot. The Umpqua Lighthouse is just a short distance north of the park and can be reached by foot. The jetty and ocean beaches can be reached by taking the road past the lighthouse.

William Tugman State Park

Location: Off Hwy 101, 10 miles south of Reedsport
Phone: 759–3604
Cost: Free/day use, $11–13/camping (April thru October)
Adjoining Eel Lake and Eel Creek, Tugman State Park offers 115 campsites (all with partial hookups) spread out among dense stands of conifer. The park's many large, flat, nicely mowed lawns give youngsters lots of space to run, play ball or frisbee, and work off a lot of energy. Other features include picnic areas and shelters, restrooms, paved trails, boat launch and fishing dock, playground, and swimming. This simple, unassuming park is often overlooked by campers searching for campsites near the ocean along the highway's west side. As

a result, space is usually available here when nearby seaside campgrounds are booked up.

Windy Cove Campgrounds A and B

Location: Salmon Harbor Dr., Winchester Bay
Cost: $7–10/camping
These two adjacent parks, protected by a hill and landscaped with trees and lawns, offer a total of 98 sites, some of which are either full or electric-only hookups. The rest are paved and rustic sites. Amenities include picnic tables, restrooms, hot showers, and playground areas. Windy Cove's access to dunes, ocean, and harbor attracts fishermen, crabbers, hikers, swimmers, and beachcombers.

Annual Events

Ocean Festival

Location: Reedsport
Date: Fourth weekend in July
Phone: 271–3495 or (800) 247–2155
On the fourth weekend of July, Reedsport explodes like a firecracker as the annual Ocean Festival gets under way. Kick-off on Friday finds the crowds heading towards four blocks of arts and crafts booths, a beer garden with live music, a quilt show, and the festival queen's coronation. Saturday opens with a bang, as the Grand Parade commences around noon. Then there are kite flying contests on the beach, old fashioned kids' games, helicopter rides, lighthouse tours, Coast Guard drills and more. Sunday's salmon dinner, held at nearby Winchester Bay, is legendary.

Kleo the Krab Bounty Hunt

Location: Reedsport
Date: Mid-August thru Labor Day
Phone: 271–3495 or (800) 247–2155
Lots of families plan their vacations for mid-August through Labor Day especially to enable them to take part in this crab

bounty hunt. Kleo the Krab (a crustacean of local fame) and 80 of his live, crabby friends and relatives are numbered, tagged and returned to Salmon Harbor. Although the event promoters provide the crabs to catch, you have to supply your own crab rings, pots, and bait. Those who catch these specially marked crabs receive a prize and commemorative Kleo T-shirt. If the so-called Kleo is caught, it's worth a cool $1,000. The event is an annual favorite for detectives of all ages who thrive on the challenge (and the prizes). The names of all those who catch tagged crabs are entered into a lottery. If by Labor Day, no one has snared Kleo for the grand prize, a drawing is held and the winner takes home ten crisp new $100 bills. This popular family activity has had winners ranging in age from nine to 75.

Section 3
South Oregon Coast

12

NORTH BEND

T he town of North Bend sits on a peninsula that juts out into Coos Bay. It was founded in 1856 by Asa Simpson as a company town for his mill and shipyard employees. But it was Louis Simpson, son of the founder, who was largely responsible for the development of North Bend. No longer the private preserve of Simpson's employees, North Bend has developed into a city of 10,000 that thrives on manufacturing, lumbering, commercial fishing, and tourism. Combined with the nearby city of Coos Bay, North Bend makes up the largest urban settlement on the entire Oregon Coast.

Sights and Attractions

All Terrain Vehicle Safety Institute

Location: 7938 East Bay Dr., North Bend
Phone: (800) 447–4700
Days/Hours: Call for schedule
Cost: $25–35/per session

Whoever dreamed going to school could be this much fun? Children as young as six can attend half-day sessions, learning all the basic techniques for safely riding all terrain vehicles (ATVs). They'll be taught on ATVs how to: start and stop, make quick turns, ride up and down steep hills, swerve, and get around obstacles. The course is a challenging one, full of the same obstacles and difficulties that ATV riders face on natural terrain. The kids will love every second of it.

Pre-registration is required. Call the number above for more information and other course locations along the Oregon Coast.

Bluebill Trail

Location: Horsfall Beach Rd., North Bend

Looping around a diminutive 40-acre lake, Bluebill Trail is one of the Oregon Coast's shortest, easiest hikes. Older children will enjoy the mix of scenic views that alternate between dunes, forest, and lake, while small youngsters will appreciate its brevity. One of the highlights is an extensive elevated board-walk system, found at about the mid-way point on the mile long trek.

Coos County Historical Museum

Location: Simpson Park, Hwy 101, North Bend
Phone: 756–6320
Days/Hours: Tues–Sat 10–4, Sun 12–4 (summer); Tues–Sat 10–4 (rest of year)
Cost: $1/adults, 25¢/ages 5–12

In front of the Coos County Historical Museum, an early 20th century steam locomotive beckons young climbers to release a little steam of their own. Upon entering this museum you'll notice a treasure chest of area history, stocked with much more than the usual arrangement of antiques and pioneer implements. The older kids will be attracted to such exquisite objects as handmade boat models of inlaid wood, a jade Chinese plaque that floated ashore after a shipwreck, a 19th century Regina Music Box, and an ornate piano shipped around Cape Horn by schooner.

Another part of the museum is devoted to a striking collection of Native American artifacts which include beaded aprons, baskets, shells, ceremonial robes, and brass thimbles. The arrowheads on display here are fascinating. At the museum's permanent hands-on exhibits, youngsters can roll up their sleeves and jump right into the pioneering spirit. They'll love handling such pioneer implements as butter churns, irons, combs, candle molds, as well as many farming and logging tools.

Frisbee Golf

Location: Simpson Park, Hwy 101, North Bend
Frisbees—don't leave home without them. That way you won't miss out on North Bend's unique golfing experience. Before arriving on the course at Simpson Park, be sure to pick up a free scorecard at Moe's Bike Shop (the last store just before the McCullough Bridge as you head north over the Coos River). Children will love the challenge of playing this course, where the "holes" are actually wire baskets affixed to brightly-colored poles. The first hole is an easy straight shot without any obstacles. But the situation takes a sinister turn as golfers proceed to successive holes along tight fairways that are laced with all sorts of "hazards."

Horsfall Beach

Location: .5 miles north of the North Bend Bridge
This wide, flat beach that seems to go on forever is ideal for running and playing, jogging, beachcombing, kite flying, surf fishing, and just plain beach walking. But that's not all. Since Horsfall Beach marks the southern boundary of the Oregon

Dunes National Recreation Area, access to these incredible dunes is as easy as a walk on the beach. Do keep an eye out however, as parts of Horsfall are open to 4-wheel drive and off-road vehicles which sometimes come roaring out of the dunes like an angry swarm of bees.

Pony Village Mall

Location: 1611 Virginia Ave., North Bend
Days/Hours: Mon–Fri 10–9, Sat 10–6, Sun 12–5

When the capricious coastal climate takes a sudden turn for the worse, it's time to go shopping. Boasting over 80 shops and services, Pony Village Mall is easily the Oregon Coast's largest enclosed mall. And while all the stores won't be of interest to kids, there are several toy, hobby, and sweets shops that'll occupy enough time while you wait for the weather to improve.

The Real Oregon Gift Myrtlewood Factory Tour

Location: 3955 Coast Hwy 101, North Bend
Phone: 756–2582
Days/Hours: Daily 8–4:30
Cost: Free tours

Although the factory tours last but a scant 15 minutes, youngsters will get to witness the transformation of raw myrtlewood into exquisitely finished pieces. Inside the cavernous 40,000 square foot factory the logs are first sawed, then carefully dried until ready to be hand crafted into finished creations. It's an interesting stop, particularly educational for older children. The younger ones will love the clamor, as saws and other buzzing power equipment cut and shape the precious wood. Guides answer questions and explain the processes and equipment seen on the tour. After the factory tour, a gift shop that's stuffed with myrtlewood products awaits.

Sand Dune Vehicle Rentals/Tours

The Oregon Dunes National Recreation Area, also known as the "Sahara-by-the-sea," is a mammoth sand box just waiting to be explored by young and old alike. And one of the best ways to do just that is by piloting your own one-person dune buggy or large 4-wheeler or by hopping aboard a dune "bus" for a wild, exhilarating tour of the dunes. Lawrence of Arabia never had it so good. All terrain vehicle (ATV) rental firms provide helmets and the necessary instructions. The minimum age for a young rider to be out without an accompanying adult varies from firm to firm and it's best to call ahead for this policy.

Far West Rentals

Location: Sandy Way, off Hwy 101; 5 miles north of North Bend
Phone: 756–2322
Days/Hours: Daily 9–dusk (summer), 11–5 (winter)
Cost: 4-wheelers: $20/hr.
Opened in 1980, Far West was the first company on the dunes to rent 4-wheelers. Discounts are available on longer-term vehicle rentals. Helmets are provided at no additional charge.

Oregon Sand Tours

Location: 9122 Wildwood Dr., North Bend
Phone: 759–4777
Days/Hours: Daily 9–dusk
Cost: Dune vehicle tours: $45/hr., $25/one-half hr.
Rates include vehicle, driver, plus up to four passengers. Reservations recommended, but drop-ins accepted. Rain gear is provided if necessary.

Pacific Coast Recreation
Location: 4121 Coast Hwy, North Bend (Hauser)
Phone: 756–7183
Days/Hours: Daily 9–dusk
Cost: Half Track tours: $12/adults, $8/under 14; 4-wheelers: $20–25/hr.
Half track tours are made inside authentic World War II military transport vehicles. Pacific Coast Recreation also conducts free showings of the coast's largest inventory of WWII and Korean war military equipment.

Spinreel Dune Buggy Rentals
Location: 9122 Wildwood Dr., North Bend
Phone: 759–3313
Days/Hours: Daily 8–8 (summer), 9–5 (winter)
Cost: Dune buggies: $18/one-half hr.; 4-wheelers: $20/one-half hr.
Offers 4 wheeler rentals for children, with parental supervision. Spinreel has a free customer shuttle service to and from the dunes enabling customers to take turns driving (and rent fewer vehicles). Also provides reduced rates for longer term rentals.

Parks and Campgrounds

Bluebill Campground
Location: Horsfall Dune and Beach Access Rd., North Bend
Phone: 271–3611
Cost: $3–5/camping
Bluebill features 20 campsites (paved tent pads) including drinking water, toilets, fireplaces, and convenient off-road vehicle access to the beach and dunes. The surrounding area teems with wildlife; it's a great place to learn about nature by observing the many songbirds, quails, foxes, hawks, shrews, beavers, and raccoons. Nearby Bluebill Lake Trail offers a pleasant, scenic, mile-long stroll around a small lake.

Annual Events

Farwest Gemcraft Show

Location: North Bend Jr. High, 1500 16th St., North Bend
Date: First weekend in August
Cost: $1/admission

For years rock hounds from all over Oregon have been coming to browse and participate in this exceptional gemcraft show. On display are outstanding works in the areas of lapidary, faceting, fossils, gems, jewelry, and crafts. The show also features competitive displays, a wheel of fortune, and an auction. Children will find the demonstrations of cutting, polishing, and engraving precious stones truly fascinating. Those wishing to take home mementos may purchase gemstones, beads, finished jewelry, rough opal, chunk rock, and carvings from any number of dealers who annually display their wares at the show.

North Bend Air Show

Location: Airport Way, North Bend Municipal Airport
Date: Mid-July
Phone: 756–1723
Cost: Free

North Bend's air show, held annually here at the south coast's largest airport, features a variety of both military and private aircraft. Adults and kids will thrill to the show's dramatic, often heart-stopping, aerial displays. Might be wise to bring a jacket along, however. Even in summer, the ocean breezes can pick up and make quite a chilly impression. Although the event officially gets underway around noon, pre-show activities usually feature a pancake breakfast. This show makes an ideal day's outing with the kids.

Oregon Hover-In

Location: Public boat launching ramp, next to North Bend Airport
Phone: (800) 824–8486 or 756–4613
Days/Hours: Mid-June
Cost: Free

Each year the Hoverclub of America transforms this site and surrounding area into a vast boisterous, hover-playground. A colorful assortment of 12 foot long hovercraft race along mud flats, rivers, beaches, and dunes a bare six inches above the surface and at speeds approaching 50 miles per hour. Kids (as well as adults) will love the hubbub—especially if they're invited by a club member to climb aboard for a demo run. It doesn't hurt to ask, especially since new members are always being sought. If you have a huge beach ball, bring it along and you might be asked to join in an outrageous match of Hovercraft water polo. You've never seen anything quite like it. For more information call the Bay Area Chamber of Commerce at the numbers above or Spinreel Dunebuggy Rentals at 759–3313.

Sandfest

Location: Horsfall Beach, North Bend
Phone: (800) 824–8486 or 756–4613
Days/Hours: First weekend in August
Cost: Free

Since 1986, Sandfest devotees have been coming to the Oregon dunes from all over the West Coast to watch or participate in exciting dune buggy and all terrain vehicle competitive events. While the Mo-to-Cross and Barrel racing events are great fun to observe, younger riders can actually take part in Potato Patch events that are especially designed for them. There's even a family riding event called Poker Runs that's as relaxed and non-competitive as anything can be. The kids will love Sandfest, and so will you. Food and souvenirs are available on site.

Southcoast Dixieland Jazz Festival

Location: Various locations in North Bend
Date: Mid-March
Phone: 269-0215

Thousands of jazz enthusiasts turn out each year to watch, listen, and tap their toes at the Southcoast Dixieland Jazz Festival. This well-organized musical extravaganza is an excellent choice for families with older children who will enjoy hearing dozens of jazz bands, shuttling (without charge) between jazz sites, attending a jazz style Gospel Service, as well as participating in the coronation of the festival King and Queen. The excitement starts early Friday evening and doesn't let up until the late night hours of Sunday. Jazz fanatics will want a three day (all events) Festival badge, admitting them to all shows at any location for the entire festival. For those not so afflicted with the jazz bug, single day events badges are available, too.

13

CHARLESTON

With its location at the mouth of Coos Bay, Charleston is home to one of Oregon's largest commercial and sport fishing fleets. Although this fishing village has an almost sleepy, Mediterranean feel to it, it's a real working town with numerous canneries and oyster farms dotting the harbor. Along with Coos Bay and North Bend, Charleston makes up what locals like to call the "Bay Area." And though Charleston may occasionally smell of fish, it's undeniably the gateway to one of the most beautiful portions of the whole Oregon Coast.

Sights and Attractions

Seven Devils Road

Location: Off Hwy 101, between Charleston and Bandon
This ten mile beach loop drive has something for everyone. Adults will enjoy the serenity and charm of the rustic countryside. Except for just a scattering of dwellings, the forested, hilly landscape shows few signs of civilization. No stores, no factories, and hardly a truck or car on the road. On the other hand,

they didn't name this roller coaster ride the Seven Devils Road for nothing. The workers who had to hack out this road across the seven deep gulches that run perpendicular to the sea probably saw Satan in their way along every foot of work. The troughs and steep hills will delight the kids—so much so, they'll be pleading with the driver to "go faster, it's more fun that way!" Seven Devils Road intersects Highway 101 just north of Bandon before crossing the Coquille River.

Shore Acres "Volkswalk"

Location: Shore Acres State Park, Charleston
What better way to see some of the coast's finest natural attractions than on foot? At least that's what the folks at the Oregon Trail State Volkssport Association think; so they designed a 10-kilometer stroll to do just that. It's a perfect family outing, covering terrain that even the youngest walkers will enjoy. Route specifics and other information can be picked up at the Davy Jones Locker Grocery in Charleston. The "peopleswalk" starts out at the park's glass-enclosed observation shelter, then proceeds across the park and up the top of a hill for a sweeping view of the rocky shoreline. Descending the hill, walkers arrive at the rugged, beautiful Cape Arago State Park. The return trip takes a route that lies along cliffs that overlook reefs, rocks, and the pounding surf. At journey's end, walkers are invited to tour the park's botanical gardens and rest awhile.

Simpson Cove

Location: Shore Acres State Park, Charleston
While most visitors to Shore Acres are content to experience the main attractions within the park itself, a few explorers venture southward for the allure of Simpson Cove. Approached from the trail just beyond the gardens at Shore Acres, Simpson cove is a sheltered inlet that offers a close-up look at waves slamming into the rocks and caves. It's the type of raw, natural display kids love to witness. They'll also enjoy exploring a small grotto at the cove's south end. But you'll have to wait for low tide to access the cave. Be sure to point out to the kids the

chunks of driftwood that have been driven into the crevices of the grotto by the awesome fury of the area's severe winter storms.

South Slough Estuary Interpretive Center
Location: Off Cape Arago Hwy on Seven Devil's Rd., Charleston
Phone: 888–5558
Days/Hours: Daily 8:30–4:30 (summer), Mon–Fri 8:30–4:30 (rest of year)
Cost: Free
Situated on a hill 300 feet above the sea, the interpretive center offers spectacular views of the South Slough Estuarine Reserve. The reserve is a 5,000 acre watershed that's incredibly productive in providing food and shelter for a wide variety of life ranging from tiny algae to great blue herons, elk, and deer. The center's exhibits explain the biological importance of the estuary, a place where fresh river waters meet the salty ocean tides. Interpreters are available to answer questions and discuss the live animals that are usually on display. Brochures describe the many offerings, including canoe tours, basketry workshops, and a children's slough safari. It's an interesting stop to make, especially for the older children who will be fascinated to learn about the dynamics of the estuary. The younger ones will certainly enjoy the guided walks and trails that lead down to the water for a close-up look.

Whale Watching Cruises
See introduction to "Whale Watching Cruises" in Chapter 7.

Betty Kay Charters
Location: Charleston Boat Basin
Phone: 888–9021 or (800) 752–6303
Days/Hours: Daily 10:30 & 1:30 (January thru June)
Cost: $20/person
Operates three hour cruises. Reservations required.

Bob's Sport Fishing

Location: Charleston Boat Basin
Phone: 888–4241
Days/Hours: Daily, call for hours (late December thru April)
Cost: $20/person
Offers three hour cruises. Reservations required. Bay excursions available upon request.

Charleston Charters

Location: 5100 Cape Arago Hwy, Charleston
Phone: 888–4846
Days/Hours: Weekends 1 pm (March thru May)
Cost: $25/person
Runs three hour cruises. Reservations required. Also provides customized bay or sea lion sightseeing cruises for groups only.

Parks and Camping

Bastendorff Beach County Park

Location: Off Cape Arago Hwy, 2 miles south of Charleston
Phone: 888–5353
Cost: $7/camping
Bastendorff offers year-round hiking, picnicking, and camping with 55 sites (includes 30 full hookups) and such amenities as wood stoves and hot showers. The beach itself is smooth, wide, and sandy. It features a rock jetty that protects the Coos River bar and makes a perfect platform from which to fish for perch or salmon. It also makes a great, long, rock pile youngsters will love to explore. In addition, the park includes a large, well-equipped playground and sandbox for the kids and great sunsets for the grown-ups.

Cape Arago State Park

Location: At end of Cape Arago Hwy, Charleston
Phone: 888–4902

For over 25 million years, the tides and winds have been chiseling away at the shoreline, and the resulting sculptured sandstone bluffs found here are unlike any others on the entire Oregon Coast. This day use park features three shallow, protected coves that are connected by short, steep trails. Young explorers will thrill to the beaches at the bottom of these trails. They're rocky with lots of tidepools, driftwood, and seaweed—just the right mix for productive beachcombing. While the historians debate whether the visit actually took place, the locals have erected a monument to commemorate the landing here by the English pirate Sir Francis Drake in the late 16th century.

Shore Acres State Park

Location: 13030 Cape Arago Hwy, Charleston
Phone: 888–4902
Situated on a high bluff overlooking the sea, Shore Acres was once the estate of lumber and shipping magnate Louis Simpson. Although the fabled mansion that once stood here was destroyed by fire in 1921, the magnificent botanical gardens remain in all their splendor. Superlatives can hardly do justice to the beauty and variety of Shore Acres. Even small children will enjoy exploring the winding paths that lead past the Japanese garden, mammoth lily pond, rose garden, and formal garden. Many of the exotic flowering trees, shrubs, and plants were brought here from the farthest corners of the world aboard Simpson's fast sailing schooners. Just as enthralling as the fragrant gardens, the dramatic vistas that can be seen from the rim of the headland here are not soon forgotten. A glass-enclosed observation station affords a stunning 180 degree view of the coast. Particularly during winter storms, the wave action below is among the most spectacular along the entire Pacific Coast.

Sunset Bay State Park

Location: Off Cape Arago Hwy, Charleston
Phone: 888–4902
Cost: Free/day use, $9–13/camping
Sunset Bay State Park offers an impressive array of day use and

overnight facilities. Day users will find picnic areas, restrooms, shelters, and after-swimming shower facilities. There are 137 campsites, 29 of which are full hookup spaces, a laundromat, and other amenities. Although the park offers such recreational diversions as fishing, boating, and hiking, what draws the most raves is the jewel-like beach. More like a semicircular lagoon, it's protected from the ocean by unique rock formations which tend to make the water both warm and calm. Without the harsh waves typically found on other Oregon Coast beaches, Sunset beach is an ideal playground for children. Its steep cliffs and natural ocean cove have long been photographed and sold to the tourist trade. Souvenir buyers may recognize this beach from the postcards they've seen in countless coastal gift shops. With its warm-waters and sheltered cove, Sunset Beach could be easily mistaken for a lagoon somewhere in Hawaii.

Annual Events

Charleston Seafood Festival
Location: Charleston Marina
Date: Mid-August
Phone: 888–2311 or (800) 824–8486
The usual serious, sedate mood of Charleston's marina gives way to hoopla and merriment as the annual fun-filled Seafood Festival gets underway. Kids of all ages will enjoy the many varied events which include a volleyball tournament, arts and crafts show, kite fly, dunk tank, and fishing pond. Prizes are raffled with proceeds benefiting local non-profit causes. A hard day of play can be rewarded by attending the seafood competition championship buffet where chefs come from all over the state to prepare delectable entrees.

Holiday Lights at Shore Acres
Location: Shores Acres State Park, Charleston
Date: December 12–31, 4–9 pm
Phone: 888–4902
For several dazzling weeks, the grounds at Shore Acres State

Park are ablaze in Christmas lights. Since 1986, the Friends of Shore Acres, a non-profit group, have been stringing up thousands of lights and inviting visitors to share in the holiday cheer. There's coffee, punch, and juices for the grown-ups and hot apple cider and cookies for the kids—all at no charge. With over 80,000 glowing bulbs and as many visitors, this delightful park that overlooks the sea becomes a magical kingdom of lights, colors, and merriment that will charm the entire family. Nightly music and Christmas caroling add to this special festive spirit.

Rhododendron Show

Location: Botanical Gardens, Shore Acres State Park, Charleston
Date: Mother's Day, 12–5 pm
Phone: 888–4902

Although rhododendrons of one variety or another seem to bloom from January through September, most are at their peak in spring and are especially spectacular around Mother's Day. Appropriately enough, the Friends of Shore Acres hold their annual rhododendron show on that day. The spectacular splashes of pinks, purples, and whites will enchant even the youngest family members. Rhododendron specialists will be conducting short talks and demonstrations of Rhododendron cultivation which some of the older members of your party may find interesting.

COOS BAY

It's very easy to get the wrong impression of Coos Bay. The route through town on Highway 101 exposes motorists to an overload of aging lumber mills and factories. And though it's one of the world's largest ports for forest products, Coos Bay has much more to offer than its industrialized core implies. This largest city on the Oregon Coast is also home to beautiful beaches, the world's largest oceanfront sand dunes, impressive parks, and a wide variety of cultural and commercial attractions. For the newcomer, the area's place names can prove a bit perplexing. Let's see if we can sort it all out. The bay in these parts is known as Coos Bay. Then there's the town of Coos Bay, which is adjacent to North Bend—both of which are contiguous with Coos Bay, the bay. Collectively, Coos Bay (the town), North Bend, and nearby Charleston refer to the piece of land they occupy as the "Bay Area." One more thing. Coos Bay (the town) was really called Marshfield for a century. It was re-named its present appellation several decades ago.

Sights and Attractions

Coast Guard Cutter Citrus

Location: On Hwy 101, Coos Bay
Phone: 269–5859
Days/Hours: Mon–Fri 3–6 pm, Sat & Sun 10–4
Cost: Free

Commissioned during World War I, this second oldest boat on active duty in the entire Coast Guard offers terrific 40-minute tours that the whole family will enjoy. Kids love bounding up the old wooden steps, crossing the gangplank and making a beeline for the gun mounts which can be handled, swiveled, and aimed (of course the ammunition has been taken out). Up on the bridge, youngsters can turn the huge steering wheel or peer out to sea through binoculars just as Coast Guard lookouts do. They can hop into the captain's seat and occasionally will get to toot the horn. The loud blast from this fog horn will get anybody's attention in a hurry. Visitors can tour the various sections of the ship including the huge galley, main deck, bridge, and even get a peek at the engine room. Displays throughout the ship explain how things work. Since the 180 foot long Citrus is a working ship that's sometimes out to sea, it's suggested that you call ahead to confirm the tour schedule.

Coast Guard Patrol Boat Orcas

Location: On Hwy 101, Coos Bay
Phone: 267–6981
Days/Hours: Mon–Fri 3–6 pm, Sat & Sun 10–4
Cost: Free

The 110 foot long Orcas, built in 1989, is a sleek, state-of-the art patrol boat that today's computer age kids will feel at home aboard. Short 20 minute tours take visitors onto the main deck, boat deck, galley, and bridge. Kids will love handling the gun mounts and navigational equipment. In stark contrast to the huge, antique steering wheel found aboard the cutter Citrus, a small joy stick is all that's needed to steer the Orcas.

As with the Citrus, the Orcas may occasionally be out on the coastal seas while you're standing at the pier waiting to climb aboard for your tour. It's best to call ahead.

Coos Art Museum

Location: 235 Anderson, Coos Bay
Phone: 267-3901
Days/Hours: Tues–Fri 11–5, Sat & Sun 1–4
Cost: $2/adults, $1/under 18
The Coos Art Museum is a must for art-minded coastal travelers *and* the only coastal art museum between San Francisco and the Canadian border. The permanent print collection is outstanding. Wander by the rotating exhibits and you might chance upon such perennial child pleasers as woodblock and metal-plate printmaking with accompanying instructional displays. The Prefontaine Memorial Sports Room exhibit is quite popular with runners and fans of the late American champion long distance runner, Steve Prefontaine, whose tragic death in a car accident in 1975 cut short a brilliant athletic career. Be sure to stop in the museum gift shop and head over to the special kid's corner where gift items have been moderately priced especially for young shoppers.

Golden and Silver Falls

Location: Coos River Rd., 24 miles east of Coos Bay
Phone: 888-3778
Though well off the beaten track, these two spectacular waterfalls have long been a popular attraction for locals and visitors alike. The last few miles of the drive are along narrow, winding roads that include some pretty steep declines. The kids will squeal with delight at this portion of the drive alone. Dropping over 200 feet, both waterfalls are impressive, thundering displays of nature at her best. The falls are particularly awesome during or after a heavy rain when the rush of water cascades with real gusto. To reach the falls, take the Allegany exit from Highway 101 and head northeast on Coos River Road. When you arrive, it's about a 60 minute, easy round trip hike to both

falls. The hike will take you through enchanted, densely forested terrain.

House of Myrtlewood

Location: 1125 S. 1st St., Coos Bay
Phone: 267–7804
Days/Hours: Daily 8–6 (summer), 8:30–5:30 (rest of year)

When you come to visit the folks at this "house" you get a guided tour of their factory. Kids love the production process where logs are cut, dried, turned, sanded, and polished—to the accompanying sights and sounds of woodworking equipment clattering away everywhere you look. After the tour, drop into their gift shop and see if you can spot some of the completed myrtlewood objects you saw being made in the factory. The House of Myrtlewood also makes their own cream and twelve varieties of butter fudge. You don't have to be a kid to get samples of your favorite kind.

Marshfield Sun Printing Museum

Location: Front St. and Hwy 101, Coos Bay
Phone: 269–1363
Days/Hours: Tues–Sat 1–4
Cost: Free

Although the Marshfield Sun newspaper shut down a half-century ago, you wouldn't know it by touring the building. Everything's been left just the way it looked on the paper's last day. Youngsters can wander through the printing office's original layout with its ancient printing presses, type cases and fonts, composing tables, large paper cutters, perforators, and other printing equipment. It's a great opportunity for parents to share a bit of bygone Americana with their computer-age youngsters. The museum's lower level has been preserved as the Marshfield Sun Newspaper and printing shop while the upper level holds a fascinating collection of vintage photos, early Marshfield and American newspapers, and exhibits on the history of printing. It's a charming look back to a distant time when newspapers were hand set and printed on hard presses.

McCullough Bridge

Location: Spanning Coos Bay

Completed in 1936, the mile-long McCullough Bridge is considered the most beautiful bridge along the entire Pacific Coast. The bridge's channel-spans clear 150 feet to allow the huge, ocean-going vessels to pass safely underneath. A pedestrian sidewalk invites a family trek across the bridge, although the frequent, nasty wind gusts might make you wish for the calm of your hotel room. However, the panoramic views from the bridge are truly breathtaking and well worth the wind-blown hike. For a different perspective take either of the graceful stairways found on each end of the bridge and head down below the massive structure.

Myrtle Point

Location: On Hwy 42, 25 miles southeast of Coos Bay

Visit Myrtle Point and leave the 20th century behind. That's the way you'll feel as you take a walking tour of the town's many historic commercial buildings and private residences that were constructed in the late 1800's.

The Logging Museum, at 7th and Maple, is housed in a 1910 church that's a smaller version of the great Mormon Tabernacle in Salt Lake City. Children will love the hands-on exhibits that include a wide variety of strange, yet fascinating, pioneer logging tools and artifacts. They'll learn through first-hand experience all about peavies, hardies, peter hooks, pickaroons, and more. Each August, Myrtle Point hosts the Coos County Fair and Rodeo; followed in September by the Harvest Festival. The December "Christmas Lights the Night" program caps yet another year of activities here. The return trip to the coast is a leisurely drive through lovely, bucolic countryside where flocks of sheep and herds of cattle seem to appear over every hill. And for those keen of eye, the journey will include glimpses of those unusual, beautiful, myrtle trees.

Parks and Camping

Mingus Park

Location: 10th & Commercial Sts., Coos Bay
Phone: 269–1181

A short walk from downtown, Mingus Park is a lovely stopping place offering beautiful Japanese gardens, picnic areas, hiking trails, as well as tennis courts, playing fields, a large swimming pool, and play equipment for youngsters. Bring plenty of duck food. Kids love to toss chunks of bread or other morsels to the ducks who usually race from the duck pond in a wild feeding frenzy to get at the handouts.

Empire Lakes Park

Location: Ackerman St., Coos Bay
Phone: 269–1181

Within the confines of the Coos Bay city limits, a 120-acre enchanted forest and lake awaits hikers, naturalists, fishermen, and young explorers. This relatively undisturbed natural area is a showplace for a wide variety of plants, trees, and animal life. The park's rich natural resources include dense forest stands, lakes, and vast grounds that are home to a rich diversity of small creatures—including deer that occasionally wander into view.

The park's easy-to-hike trails are paved or packed gravel and provide pleasant woodsy walks around the lakes. While non-motorized boating, swimming, and fishing are popular lake activities, just running across all the foot bridges here can be plenty of fun, too.

Annual Events

Bay Area Fun Festival

Location: Downtown Coos Bay
Date: Third weekend in September
Phone: (800) 824–8486 or 269–0215
One of the area's largest festivals kicks off with a collection of sights, sounds, and smells certain to grab the fancy of everyone in the family. The Bay Area Fun Festival features a parade, international food booths, arts and crafts, live bands, dancers, and non-stop entertainment throughout the weekend. The teen dance is a favorite with the older youngsters, while the smaller children enjoy the wandering clowns and the children's carnival. Probably the most popular children's activity is the "Pre for Kids," (named after the area's famous runner, Steve Prefontaine) where youngsters in grades one through eight compete in fun runs and T-shirts and hats are given to all participants. A half dozen other scheduled events, including tours of a U.S. Navy ship docked at the downtown waterfront help make this festival a terrific event for all.

Blackberry Arts Festival

Location: Downtown Mall, Coos Bay
Date: Fourth Saturday in August
Phone: 267–7232
Have no doubts. Blackberries are serious business along the coast in these parts. So much so, that for the past ten years the annual Blackberry Arts Festival has been whipping up a sea of blackberry pies, blackberry scones, blackberry shakes, and other blackberry treats for festival goers. Besides the everpresent blackberry, the festival features works of art by Oregon artists and craftspeople. Many of these highly talented individuals will be demonstrating their techniques at their booths. Kids love seeing how things are done. They'll also enjoy the special spinning and weaving demonstrations. In addition, the nearby Coos Art Museum will once again hold

organized children's art activities. To add to all these festivities, there are strolling musicians, clog dancers, and meandering singers.

Oregon Coast Music Festival

Location: Various Coos Bay locations
Date: Last two weeks in July
Phone: 267–0938
Cost: Varies by event; some free

The Oregon coast is the perfect backdrop for the Music Festival's annual presentation of fine musical offerings. Concerts feature classical, jazz, bluegrass, big band sounds, Broadway show tunes, and light classical themes. It's a gala event that will be enjoyed especially by those who are musically-inclined. With so many concert choices, parents and kids can select the music suited to their individual tastes.

The free outdoor picnic concerts in the park, with the ocean undulating in the distance, are particularly pleasant family outings. Besides Coos Bay, the Oregon Coast Music Festival takes place at various locations in North Bend, Bandon, and Reedsport.

15

BANDON

After a devastating fire that destroyed most of the city in 1936, Bandon has rebounded to become a popular vacation spot and artist colony. It's an attractive town that has a character and charm reminiscent of an earlier, genteel period. Perhaps no better place in Bandon typifies this elegance than Old Town, where cafes, craft shops, galleries, historic buildings, theaters, and live music all look out upon a picturesque, active harbor. Bandon's natural beauty is no less awesome than is its urban renaissance. Piercing the Pacific, natural rock formations stand like statues at watch over smooth, sandy beaches that are as fine as they come. The Coquille River, many parks, and beaches attract large numbers of beachcombers, sportfishermen, hikers, campers, and outdoor enthusiasts. And when the weather turns nasty, monstrous waves furiously smash against the rocky coastline, earning Bandon the title: "Storm Watching Capital of the World."

Sights and Attractions

Bandon Cheese Factory
Location: On Hwy 101, just north of Old Town, Bandon
Phone: (800) 548–8961
Days/Hours: Daily 8:30–5:30
Cost: Free
They're still making cheddar cheese by hand here, just as it's been done for the past sixty years. Young visitors enjoy watching the cheese-making process through glass windows. Large, brick cheese curds can be seen being flipped over and over in long stainless steel vats to allow the liquid whey to drain off. The slabs are next sent through shredders, then pressed overnight and stored for the important aging process to start. There's also a short video covering the whole process, from cow to cheese. Be sure to take advantage of the generous "factory direct" cheese samples offered.

Bandon Historical Society Museum
Location: W. 1st St., Bandon
Phone: 347–2164
Days/Hours: Tues–Sat 10–4
Cost: 50¢/adults, free/under 12
The Old Coast Guard Building along Bandon's waterfront is home to a fascinating collection of memorabilia from Bandon's early days. The permanent display on the Coquille Indians is rich in native artifacts including exquisite basketry, fishing tools, and cooking gear. Older youngsters will be intrigued by the exhibits and photos that grimly deal with the area's devastating fires, shipwrecks, and Coast Guard lifesaving efforts along the dangerous Coquille River bar. Before-and-after fire photos and newspaper accounts of the 1936 conflagration are sober reminders of Bandon's tragic past. On a lighter note, several exhibit rooms celebrate the town's famous cranberry reputation and early years when it was known as the "Playground of the Pacific."

Bandon Riding Stables

Location: 2747 Beach Loop Dr., Bandon
Phone: 347–9181
Days/Hours: Daily, call for hours
Cost: $15 hr.

What kid wouldn't love horseback riding on beach trails and over sand dunes? For the even smaller set there are pony rides and wagon rides along the beach. After just a few lessons provided by the staff, even beginners will be able to hit the trails a la The Lone Ranger. Bandon Riding Stables also offers sunset rides and overnight pack trip rides by reservation only.

Bandon Storm Watchers Programs

Location: Hwy 101 at 11th St., Bandon Community Center
Phone: 347–9616
Days/Hours: Saturdays 3 pm (January thru April)
Cost: Free

To better appreciate Bandon's winter, timber-rattling coastal storms, the Bandon Storm Watchers have put together a series of informative programs on the weather and other natural phenomena that adults and older children will find both fascinating and fun. Youngsters and oldsters will be taught the ins and outs of beachcombing, whale watching, tidepooling, birding, wild flowering, and of course, storm watching. Caution: after attending a few programs you might find yourself forsaking a warm, dry hotel room to stand on the shore, thrilling to the crashing waves and fury of a stormy sea.

Beach Loop Drive

Location: Off Hwy 101, West of Bandon

This scenic loop along the bluffs southwest of town reveals panoramic vistas of fantastic offshore rock formations—remnants of a prehistoric coastline. From Rock Face Viewpoint you'll see such giant carvings as Elephant Rock, Table Rock, Garden of the gods, and Cat and Kittens Rocks. Resembling the head of a sleeping man, Race Rock was created by the battering tides over tens of thousands of years. Indian legends disagree. Face Rock, they say, is the remains of an ancient mariner frozen by an evil sea god. A hike down the steep trails to the water reveals deserted beaches that are ideal for young beachcombers and tidepool explorers. Driftwood, agates, and an amazing variety of birdlife are typically encountered during a stroll along the shoreline.

Coquille River Lighthouse

Location: Hwy 101 and Bullards Beach Rd., 1 mile north of Bandon
Days/Hours: Daily, dawn to dusk (summer only)
Cost: Free

In its day, the Coquille River Lighthouse was known as the "Guardian" of that particularly perilous spot where the Coquille River meets the ocean. So perilous, that in 1903 a great storm actually rammed a schooner into the lighthouse itself. Although no longer functional, the lighthouse has been refurbished and stocked with exhibits and photographs to commemorate the 1903 accident as well as other shipwrecks. It's a fascinating look at some of the ships that made it across Bandon's treacherous bar, and those that didn't. The Lighthouse can be reached along the road that parallels the Coquille River as it races through Bullards Beach State Park to empty into the sea.

Cranberry Bog Tours

Location: Contact Bandon Visitor Center for locations
Phone: 347-9616

Although you won't be able to jump into the cranberry bogs for a hands-on experience, just watching the growers harvest these crimson, juicy berries is quite a treat. The youngsters will love watching growers wade into the flooded cranberry beds to mechanically shake the berries from the submerged vines. Floating to the top, the berries are corralled by long wooden booms into tight concentrations resembling plush red carpet. Next, the berries are pushed towards submerged hoppers then lifted by conveyors to waiting trucks. Ask to try on a pair of the grower's specially designed stilt shoes (wooden platforms fastened by short wooden pegs to the soles of the boots). They're worn in the bogs to keep from trampling the berries. The most interesting times to visit are during the late autumn harvests.

Cranberry Sweets Company
Location: 1st St., Bandon
Phone: 347–2526
Days/Hours: Daily 9–5
A visit to Bandon, the heralded "Cranberry Capital of the West," would not be complete without a visit to Cranberry Sweets. Age doesn't matter here; only a sweet tooth is required. The collection of cranberry-flavored sweets is truly awesome, ranging from cranberry candy and cakes to cranberry fudge and truffles. For those who can't seem to make up their minds, free samples are generously doled out. A short video on cranberry harvesting will explain what's in all those reddish-tinged fields you see along the highway around Bandon.

Old Town
Location: Opposite the docks in Bandon
Large handcrafted arches stand before Old Town Bandon, beckoning visitors to explore the wonderful collection of shops, eateries, museums, and even candy factories found here. A self-guided walking tour (you can pick up a brochure from the Visitors Bureau at the entrance of Old Town) is a great way for parents to share with their children the town's colorful history. For the younger set, a stop at both the Fudge Factory and Cranberry Sweets (yes, free cranberry candy and fudge samples are offered) is a must. Inside the Big Wheel Farm Supply a driftwood museum features a bizarre collection of natural wood sculptures that imaginative youngsters will find fascinating.

Some of Old Town's treasures are not as readily visible as others. Tucked away in many of its historic buildings are artisans and craftspeople busy at work in pottery making, leathercrafting, and glassblowing—often as visitors watch.

Professional Sports Hall of Fame

Location: On Hwy 101, 7 miles south of Bandon
Phone: 347–9131
Days/Hours: Daily 10–5
Cost: $2/adults, $1/14 years & under

Sports legends from the worlds of basketball, baseball, and football will come alive as you wander through this unique museum. Over 3,000 authentic player jerseys, including caps, gloves, helmets, balls, bats, and jackets, many autographed, are on display here. Rounding out this impressive collection are nearly 5,000 large, autographed photos of sports greats. Though the museum is undeniably packed to the rafters with sports memorabilia, it's the jerseys that steal the show. Fans of all ages will get a real kick out of seeing the actual, game-worn shirts from such greats as Larry Bird, Darryl Strawberry, Joe Montana, Willie Mays, Pete Rose, Sandy Koufax, Roberto Clemente, and many others.

West Coast Game Park

Location: On Hwy 101, 6 miles south of Bandon
Phone: 347–3106
Days/Hours: Daily 9–dusk (March thru November), hours vary (rest of year)
Cost: $5.75/adults, $4.50/7–12 year olds, $3.25/2–6 year olds

The next best thing to an African safari—a stroll through the West Coast Game Park—will bring you a face-to-face encounter with hundreds of free-roaming animals and birds. Kids will love the chance to be close to so many creatures, and most especially to feed and pet them. Holding and cuddling the many cubs, pups, and kits is enough to bring out the kid in any grown-up. The park's large predators and big hooved animals are housed in special exhibits which keep visitors safely at arms-length. A souvenir and gift shop are also on the premises.

Whiskey Run Beach

Location: Along Seven Devils Rd., 2 miles north of Bandon

Walk along this fine beach and run your hands through the sand. In another time you might have noticed flakes of gold. It was along the beaches here, almost 150 years ago, that these gold-bearing sands launched a gold rush down Oregon's south coast. Kids are easily convinced that there's gold left for them to find if only their parents would give them a little time to sift enough sand. Nowadays, what Whiskey Run Beach lacks in precious ore it makes up in miles of quiet, solitary shoreline. A perfect adult's escape from the cares of the world, and a remarkably fertile place for young beachcombers and agate-hunters. The clamming is exceptional.

The Wool Company
Location: 990 2nd St., Bandon
Phone: 347–3912
Days/Hours: Call for hours
This shop stocks wool in every possible shape and color, from raw fleeces and yarns to completed garments, blankets, and rugs. You'll have to hold on to small children as they'll be sorely tempted by the colorful inventory to jump right in and get involved. There's a large display of spinning wheels, looms, weavers tools, and exotic yarns and fibers. For those wishing to learn, The Wool Company provides modestly-priced lessons in the art of spinning, weaving, and knitting. Ask to have a try at a spinning wheel. They'll gladly show you how. Even the little ones will be fascinated to watch shop employees putting together spinning wheels.

Parks and Camping

Bullards Beach State Park
Location: On Hwy 101, 1 mile north of Bandon
Phone: 347–2209
Cost: Free/day use, $9–13/camping
Although the park's 192 campsites and other camping facilities are quite good, it's the day use part of Bullards Beach that deserves the accolades. Within the park you'll find miles of ocean and river beaches, low sand dunes, and plenty of open, wide, grassy lawns. It's a great place for kids to fly kites, explore

dunes, beachcomb, play on the playground equipment, or just plain loll about in the beautifully landscaped parkland along the wide river that cuts through this park. A paved, level walkway follows the river to the sea about a mile away.

Annual Events

Cranberry Festival
Location: Downtown Bandon
Date: Mid-September
Phone: 347-9616
Bandon's famous fruit is celebrated in a gala three-day festival that's packed with activities—and thousands of visitors and locals, too. The Cranberry Food Fair pits scores of homemade cranberry delights against one another and free samples are the order of the day. The Cranberry Queen's coronation and ball, a parade with floats, an arts and crafts show, and a volleyball tournament are a few of the highlights. The young crowd will enjoy the roving clowns, mounted horse routines, kite-flying contest, and artisans demonstrating their talents. The Cranberry Festival has enough variety to please all members of the family.

Sandcastle and Sculpture Competition
Location: Seabird Land at Beach Loop Rd., Bandon
Date: Last weekend in May
Phone: 347-9616
Although the sand creations are all complete and ready for judging at 1 p.m., the best time to watch is around 8 a.m. when the construction begins. If you care to join in, the contest is open to individuals or groups, from pre-schoolers to grown-ups. The only requirement is that nothing but sand, water, and creativity go into each sand sculpture. Whether they're merely watching the action unfold, or actually pitching in to create an award-winning sandcastle, children are fascinated by this event.

16

PORT ORFORD

Port Orford is a gem-like coastal town nestled along scenic bluffs overlooking the Pacific. It's endowed with deep forests, turquoise rivers, freshwater lakes, and a "banana belt" climate that allows gardens to bloom all year. Unlike most other coastal towns, Port Orford has no river, so the town's harbor lies directly on the sea. This gives its fishing fleet the advantage of having no hazardous river bar to cross en route to port. Port Orford was established in 1851 on the site of one of the fiercest Indian battles ever pitched along the Oregon Coast. Nearly a century earlier, British Captain George Vancouver sighted the bluffs here and named the area after his friend, the Earl of Orford. One more thing about Port Orford: it's the most westerly incorporated city in the continental U.S. You just can't go much farther west and stay on the mainland.

Sights and Attractions

Elk River Hatchery

Location: 7 miles off Hwy 101, on Elk River Rd., Port Orford
Phone: 332-7025
Days/Hours: Daily 8-4 (July thru September)

Birthplace to nearly a million chinook salmon and steelhead trout each year, the Elk River Hatchery is a terrific visit for all members of the family. The hatchery, operated by the Oregon Department of Fish and Wildlife, spawns the fish then releases them into rivers. The fish will eventually wind up in the ocean, grow to adulthood, then return to the exact same river where they began their life's journey. The purpose for all this is to provide recreation for sports anglers and livelihoods for commercial fishermen.

Feeding time at the hatchery is unlike any luncheon at your house. Even little children will love watching as tens of thousands of tiny fish all compete for their portion of the grub. The twice-daily feedings always draw choruses of oohs and aahs from crowds of excited youngsters. Another popular viewing event occurs throughout September when the minute fish are gently vacuumed up by pumps for delivery to rivers or streams. In addition, visitors may watch as fish biologists and hatcherymen select fish eggs, treat fish for diseases, and maintain the hatchery ponds and facilities. It's an interesting stop, particularly educational for older children.

Floras Lake

Location: Just west of Langlois, 13 miles north of Port Orford

Separated from the ocean by a narrow strip of stable dune sand, Floras Lake is a small fresh-water lake fluttering with windsurfers. Although the youngsters will enjoy just standing on the beach watching the colorful windsurfers fly by, they'll absolutely thrill to the chance to try it themselves. And, fortuitously, the Floras Lake Windsurfing School is right there to teach spirited kids and adults how to capture the wind and fly over the whitecaps. All you need is a bathing suit and some sneakers that you don't mind getting water-logged; the school supplies all the rest. For more details call the school at 347–9205.

Garrison Lake

Location: West of Hwy 101, on 12th St., Port Orford

Garrison Lake is probably Port Orford's best kept secret. The lake is a beautiful, tranquil body of clear water that's home to an amazing variety of wildlife. Children will enjoy the chance to explore a real wilderness and see otter, deer, raccoons, beaver, hawks, and scores of different species of birdlife at home in the surrounding marsh, meadow, and forest land. This secluded, uncrowded recreational jewel also offers day users picnic tables, restrooms, a boat launch, and a floating dock. For those few who venture forth to discover it, Garrrison Lake makes an ideal day's outing.

Hughes House Museum

Location: At Cape Blanco State Park, 8 miles north of Port Orford

Phone: 332–2975

Days/Hours: Mon, Thurs & Sat 10–5; Sun 12–5 (May thru September)

Cost: Free

A fine example of coastal Victorian architecture, the historic Hughes House invites visitors to come inside and travel back in time nearly a century. Especially for older, imaginative children, this museum brings to life a golden era in the late 19th century. A wealth of antique furnishings and photographs fills this completely restored home that was once the showpiece of a 1,000 acre dairy ranch. Hughes House is also the site of a variety of summer activities including wool spinning and crocheting demonstrations, a vintage car exposition, and more.

Port of Port Orford

Location: Off Hwy 101, Port Orford

Port Orford's unique open harbor offers several interesting

dockside activities the whole family will enjoy. In late afternoons the dock is animated with the return of fishing boats carrying the day's catch. Youngsters will be captivated by the sight of ships being unloaded and fish being counted, weighed, boned, and cleaned for market. A truly awesome sight to see is a vessel suspended in mid-air. It's not a supernatural phenomenon, just one of the dock's heavy duty boat hoists lifting a ship from the ocean for storage or returning one back to the sea for action. In winter, visitors are treated to the amazing spectacle of ships of the fishing fleet, some weighing up to 15 tons each, being hoisted effortlessly from the ocean onto dockside trailers to escape the season's battering, stormy seas. Even the locals never tire of watching the port hoist in action.

Prehistoric Gardens

Location: On Hwy 101, 12 miles south of Port Orford
Phone: 332–4463
Days/Hours: Daily 8–dusk
Cost: $4.50/adults, $3.50/ages 12–18, $2.50/ages 5–11

For nearly forty years, visitors have been entering Prehistoric Gardens and leaving the modern world behind. A natural rain forest, replete with luxuriant ferns, huge moss-covered trees, and creeks and streams, is the setting for dozens of huge, lifelike models of dinosaurs and other prehistoric creatures. Children will be awed by the enormous size of the weird beasts lurking in the jungle forest. While strolling along a quiet path, a sudden confrontation with a 50-foot tall brachiosaurus is enough to grab anyone's attention. A bit farther, one encounters an ancient turtle, larger than a truck. Each exhibit comes with its own unobtrusive plaque containing enough factual information to satisfy any young natural scientist's curiosity. Prehistoric Gardens is an educational (and highly entertaining) exposition recommended by several national magazines and newspapers as well as by many youngsters who sum it up in one word: "Awesome." A gift and souvenir shop features unusual items that relate to prehistoric animals.

Stone Butte Stables

Location: 46509 Hwy 101, 8 miles north of Port Orford
Phone: 348–2525
Days/Hours: Daily 10–6 (May thru September)
Cost: $12/per hr.

Stone Butte Stables offers horseback rides into the Oregon Coast foothills that every member of the family will enjoy. Trails wind through an 800 acre preserve of forests, meadows, and streams. The area is rich in wildlife, and youngsters are delighted to spot deer, raccoons, snakes, and bears. For those seeking more of a western adventure, the sunset barbecue ride may be just the thing. Riders leave the stables a few hours before sundown. After an easy hour's ride, an ocean view campsite is reached where a crackling campfire and waiting barbecue beckon riders to dismount and relax. After a hearty meal around the fire, riders return to the stables in the last light of day. It's an adventure the family will long treasure.

Parks and Camping

Battle Rock Park

Location: On the beach, at the south end of Port Orford
Fronting the shoreline is an immense monolith that was once the scene of possibly the bloodiest, fiercest Indian battle ever waged along the entire Oregon Coast. In June 1851 a small landing party of white settlers made camp on Battle Rock. Almost immediately, Indians attacked and were repulsed in vicious hand to hand combat. The settlers wisely had brought a small cannon whose lethal fire proved fatal to any hopes the Indians had for success. A month later, reinforcements arrived by sea to carry the day. A fort was built and the settlement of Port Orford was established. Older children will be awed to stand on the site of the battle, which is described in great detail on an historical marker at the park. Even young children will wish to climb this immense rock promontory. Battle Rock can be approached from the beach along a foot trail that leads to the top—where bracing winds, dazzling coastal views, and ghosts of the past await.

Buffington Park

Location: 14th St., in central Port Orford

This delightful 20-acre city park has something for every member of the family, including picnic tables, a Swiss paracourse for exercise buffs, a jogging trail, a ball field, tennis and basketball courts, and new playground equipment. Although there's a full complement of slides and swings here, what really sparkles is a small commercial fishing boat that's been de-commissioned for the exclusive use of junior sailors. The children will love to climb aboard, jump overboard, and "pilot" this land locked ship all over the world without ever leaving sight of their picnicking parents. The park adjoins a small lake that offers a fine swimming hole in summer. With many winding trails and plenty of room to run and play, Buffington makes a perfect place for the whole family to unwind.

Cape Blanco State Park

Location: Off Hwy 101, 9 miles north of Port Orford
Phone: 332–6774
Cost: Free day use, $9–13/camping (April thru October)

The conifer-sheltered campground (58 sites with partial hookups) sits on a high windswept bluff affording stunning ocean views. A bit upstream along the Sixes River, the day use area provides a pleasant spot for a family outing with such amenities as picnic sites, water, restrooms, and a boat launch for river access. Cape Blanco offers superb ocean views, a first rate black sand beach, fine hiking, wildlife watching, and fishing. In addition, there's the Hughes House Museum (see description in this chapter) and the oldest, highest lighthouse still in use on the Oregon Coast.

Incidentally, young history buffs like to know that the Cape Blanco Lighthouse was used during World War II by Japanese submarines as an orientation point to aim planes armed with firebombs. Their intent was to start massive forest fires to disrupt the American war effort. But the damp climate won out over the few incendiary bombs that were actually dropped on nearby Mt. Avery and Mt. Emily. Other historical sites within the park will also appeal to older children. The remnants of a cemetery and church used by the area's early settlers, and the black sand beach gold-mining operation are places well worth exploring.

Humbug Mountain State Park

Location: Off Hwy 101, 6 miles south of Port Orford
Phone: 332–6774
Cost: Free/day use, $9–13/camping (April thru October)
The park's 107 campsites (including 30 full-hookups) and separate day use area hug the base of Humbug Mountain in a lush forest that surrounds a verdant meadow and tranquil stream. Picnic sites, water, and restrooms are a few of the typical amenities visitors will find. Although the fishing and swimming are excellent, the hiking opportunities really stand out. A three mile hike on Humbug Mountain Trail, appropriate for older youngsters, leads through dense forest to the crest of Humbug Mountain. Kids will enjoy the eerie, often spooky trail portions that seem to wind deep into a forest so thick that much of the daylight is blocked out. The trek is also notable for the chance to observe an abundance of wildlife in the area; hikers often surprise small animals darting across the path. Another trail, an easy five minute stroll, leads from camp to an attractive beach along the seacoast. Yet another twists and turns within the park, crossing footbridges and providing even the smallest children with great places to explore.

Annual Events

Port Orford Arts Fest

Location: Various locations in town
Date: First weekend in May
Phone: 332–8055
Celebrating the visual and performing arts and crafts, Port Orford's Arts Festival is the largest event of its kind on the Oregon Coast. From one end of Port Orford to the other, a variety of colorful, vibrant displays and demonstrations will captivate all members of the family. Youngsters will be de-

lighted as the glassblowers and potters playfully demonstrate their talents with whimsical child-pleasing creations. Kids and adults will watch in fascination as basket weavers, quilt makers, wool spinners, woodworkers, and silversmiths all carry on craft traditions dating back hundreds of years. Last but not least, taste buds of all ages are sure to be stimulated by the gourmet food tasting exhibitions.

Port Orford Jubilee

Location: Battle Rock Park and various locations
Date: July 4th, 8 am–10 pm
Phone: 332–8055

The celebration of American Independence is a major family event in Port Orford. The sandcastle building contest and kite flying contest will appeal to kids of all ages. A parade with numerous marching bands, clowns, the Sheriff's Posse, and other colorful horse riders will thrill even the smallest children. Also featured are a fish-box derby, a dinghy race (a truly wild event!), horse games, and clog dancing demonstrations. A stirring event is the reenactment of the historic battle that took place at Battle Rock nearly 150 years ago. Settlers and Indians fought a bloody skirmish there resulting in the defeat and banishment of the Indians from the area. An extraordinary fireworks display follows at dusk at Battle Rock Park. The adjacent hills provide an excellent natural amphitheater for spectacular viewing.

17

GOLD BEACH

N amed for the gold that early prospectors found in the dark sandy beaches and seaward bluffs, Gold Beach today is the hub for many coastal and river recreational activities. The town's legendary Rogue River has long been famous for its salmon and steelhead; anglers come from around the world to try their luck in the Rogue. Of course the river has also gained fame from the dynamic jet boats that whisk passengers more than 50 miles upriver. With beachcombing, clamming, crabbing, year-round warm weather, gorgeous scenery, secluded beaches, and tourist attractions and events, Gold Beach has enough to keep any visitor busy for days.

Sights and Attractions

Cape Sebastian

Location: Off Hwy 101, 7 miles south of Gold Beach
Days/Hours: Daily, dawn to dusk

Whether you're heading up or down the coast, don't pass up this spectacular headland. Rising 700 feet above the sea, towering Cape Sebastian affords absolutely stunning ocean views— on a clear day you can see 50 miles in either direction. It's a breathtaking, beautiful hilltop site that will bewitch even small children. A paved hiking trail leads along the ridge to other sensational overlooks. Far below, strangely shaped rocks and mini-islands can be seen poking through the water, taking a constant beating from the crashing waves. The drive to the cape top is a thrilling experience in its own right—at least the children will think so. Young back-seat drivers will chirp with glee as mom or dad negotiates the narrow, very steep access road to the top, at times coming perilously close to the edge. It's a drive not for the faint of heart or for overloaded or underpowered automobiles.

Curry County Historical Museum

Location: 920 S. Ellensburg, Gold Beach Fairgrounds
Phone: 247–6113
Days/Hours: Daily 1–5 (summer), Fri & Sat 12–4 (rest of year)
Cost: Free

This small, but well organized, museum has good exhibits on Indian and pioneer life and gold mining, as well as musical instruments, vintage photos, and maritime displays. Kids will be especially interested in the realistic reproduction of the interior of a gold miner's cabin. In addition, outdoor exhibits feature several extraordinary artifacts, including an Indian log canoe over 250 years old, and boulders retrieved from Rogue River canyons containing mysterious old Indian petroglyphs. The Curry County Historical Museum is a fine place for children to learn of the people and events that occupied another time in the history of a small corner of our nation.

Jerry's Rogue River Museum

Location: At the Port of Gold Beach
Phone: 247–4571 or (800) 451–3645
Days/Hours: Daily 8–8 (May thru October); Mon–Sat 9–5, Sun 12–5 (rest of year)
Cost: Free

Before hopping aboard a jet boat for an exhilarating adventure up the Rogue, stop at this museum first to make the river journey even more enjoyable. Housed within is a vast collection of artifacts, photos, and graphics showing the geological formation of the Rogue, early settlers and river travel, and local history. It's an interesting visit and particularly educational for older children. But even the younger set will be attracted to the natural history exhibit which features stuffed birds, animals, and fish all realistically displayed in their natural habitat. In addition, the display of old rifles and Indian arrowheads holds the interest of most kids and adults.

Indian Creek Trail Rides

Location: Jerry's Flat Rd., Gold Beach
Phone: 247–7704
Days: Daily (May thru September)
Cost: Call for rates

One and two hour guided trail rides are available for horseback tours of the scenic coastal mountains high above the Rogue River Valley. The rides depart several times a day. The lunch ride will appeal to the younger riders who get to ride a bit, then stop for chow. You hit the trail at 11 am, ride for about an hour, then dismount by Indian Creek for a sack lunch that's provided for each rider. Following this feast by the creek, you hit the trail for the hour return to the stables. Call for rates and departure times. Reservations are required.

Rogue River Jet Boat Trips

For those not opposed to blasting their way through the wilderness, the best way to experience the wild Rogue is aboard a jet-powered boat. Accompanied by the whine of the jet engine, you "fly" along the river faster than a speeding bullet. Several companies operate boat trips, offering round trips that vary in length from 64 to 104 miles. Most people who "do" the Rogue opt for the shorter trips. However, those taking the longer ones are rewarded by the entry into a 13 mile wilderness segment of the river notable for its pristine scenery, thrilling whitewater, and canyon walls that rise 1,500 feet above. Jet boats, many with more than a thousand horsepower of hydrojet, skim the river's surface and can be easily maneuvered in a mere few inches of water. Pilots frequently stop to describe the history and scenery of the area and to thrill their audience with closeup views of deer, beavers, bears, and other wildlife. It's best to wear layered clothing that can be shed, since the temperatures will rise dramatically the farther upriver you get from the ocean.

Jerry's Rogue Jets

Location: Gold Beach Boat Basin
Phone: 247–4571 or (800) 451–3645
Days/Hours/Cost: See below
From May through October Jerry's runs a 64-mile roundtrip and a 104-mile roundtrip up the Rogue. The shorter trip lasts six hours and departs daily at 8:30 a.m. From July through Labor Day additional departures are at 2:30 p.m. Adults pay $25, kids four to eleven pay $20. The eight-hour, 104 mile whitewater trip departs daily at 8 a.m. and also at noon, July through Labor Day. Adults pay $50, kids four to eleven pay $20. Jerry's has been in the business for over thirty years, and also offers other tours and cruises on the Rogue and bay.

Mail Boat Hydro-Jets

Location: Mail Boat Dock, .25 miles upstream from Rogue River Bridge
Phone: 247–7033 or (800) 458–3511
Days/Hours/Cost: See below
Mail Boat offers Rogue River roundtrips of 64 miles, 80 miles, and 104 miles generally from May through Octo-

ber. The 64 mile trip leaves at 8:30 a.m. each day (also at 2:30 p.m. from July through Labor Day). Adults pay $25, those four to eleven pay $10. The 80-mile whitewater trips operate daily only from mid-June through mid-September. Departures are at 8 a.m. and 2:30 p.m. with adult fares at $37.50, and $15 for those ages four to eleven. Daily eight-hour trips of 104 miles depart at 8 a.m. (no afternoon departures) and cost $50 for adults, and $20 for those four to eleven. Their new glass enclosed excursion boats allow for comfortable sightseeing in any weather, rain or shine. Besides tourists, these mail boats actually do carry mail to the town of Agness and other towns farther inland.

Wild Bill's Jet Boat Rides
Location: 30401 Hillside Terrace, Gold Beach
Phone: 247–2671
Days/Hours/Cost: See below
80 mile roundtrip whitewater river rides depart daily at 8:30 a.m. and 2:30 p.m. in summer. Adults pay $50, while those 12 and under pay $25. Special all-day excursion charters are available for $500. You get the boat and pilot for ten hours and can bring along up to six passengers. They'll take you and your party wherever you want to go; stop as long as you like—it's your boat for the day.

Rogue-Pacific Interpretive Center
Location: 510 Colvin St., Gold Beach
Phone: 247–6023
Days/Hours/Cost: Call for specifics
The Rogue-Pacific Interpretive Center is a private, nonprofit association that offers a variety of educational and recreational activities that highlight the south coast's remarkable environment. The whole family will thoroughly enjoy whizzing along aboard jet boats to observe seals and sea lions off the coast, going on tidepooling expeditions to see what's lurking and crawling around, learning how to catch steelhead or how to find and dig clams, exploring the county's early gold

mines, and engaging in a number of other captivating pursuits. Younger children will be delighted by the special kids' programs on whales, seals, and forest wildlife. Who says learning can't be fun—great fun? For information on classes or a brochure, call the center at the number above.

Parks and Camping

Arizona Beach Resort
Location: Off Hwy 101, 14 miles north of Gold Beach
Phone: 332–6491
Cost: $8 and up/camping
Choices abound at this large private campground. You can camp on the beach, in an adjoining meadow, or in a forest by a small, gurgling stream. There's no shortage of things for children to do. The private beach is heavily strewn with every imaginable size and shape of driftwood. In addition, an abundance of brilliantly colored stones makes the shoreline a paradise for driftwood and agate combers. Other activities include surf fishing, hiking, and swimming. Youngsters will also delight in playing in and around a creek that peacefully meanders through the resort on its way to the sea.

Quosatana Campground
Location: Jerry's Flat & Agness Rd., Gold Beach
Phone: 247–6651
Cost: $5/camping (April thru November)
The 43 campsites (no hookups) at this USDA Forest Service campground are nestled in a stunningly beautiful forest setting. Provided are such basics as picnic tables at each widely separated space, restrooms, water, and boat ramps for access to the adjoining Rogue River. Of special interest to children are rocky river beaches that are perfect for rock hounding and beachcombing. Nearby, sandy bottomed swimming holes will entertain youngsters for hours. This is a fine family campground; the water and woods provide plenty of opportunities for relaxing, playing, and exploring.

18

BROOKINGS

While it's unlikely you'll ever find bananas growing in Brookings, the town's mild year round climate has earned it the billing: "The Banana Belt" of the Oregon Coast. Locals never tire of pointing out that in winter while Brookings basks in the grip of dramatic warm spells, much of the rest of Oregon shivers. This complex meteorological phenomenon is best left for the chamber of commerce to try to explain. Brookings, and the adjoining town of Harbor, offer outdoors enthusiasts many fine opportunities for hiking, boating, fishing, camping, and beachcombing. Additional scenic attractions include gorgeous state parks and world renowned lily fields, home to 90% of all the lilies grown in America.

Brookings is also remembered for a bizarre attack that occurred in September 1942. It was then that a Japanese war plane, assembled off the coast aboard a Japanese submarine, dropped incendiary bombs in a forest just east of town near Mount Emily. Fortunately, Oregon's damp coastal climate and lush forestland thwarted the conflagration hoped for by the attackers. It is the only spot on the United States mainland to have suffered an enemy aerial attack during WWII.

Sights and Attractions

Chetco Valley Museum

Location: Museum Rd., Brookings
Phone: 469–6651
Days/Hours: Wed–Sun 12–5 (summer), Thurs–Sun 12–4 (rest of year)
Cost: Free

High on a hill overlooking Highway 101, an older red and white building valiantly holds on to the past. Dating back to the early 19th century, the structure was used as a stagecoach stop and trading post long before Abraham Lincoln was elected President. Inside the museum, visitors will discover a collection of pioneer artifacts including furnishings, tools, a spinning wheel, old sewing machines, and many other mementos. Several exceptional displays will pique the interest of older children. These include a small trunk brought around Cape Horn in 1706, a collection of early 20th century Japanese swords, Indian arrowheads, and an ancient dugout canoe. Perhaps the most intriguing exhibit is an iron casting of a woman's face. It has been suggested that it is a likeness of Queen Elizabeth, a relic left behind by Sir Francis Drake when he visited the coast on one of his journeys in 1579.

Upon leaving the museum for your return to the present, wander over to a corner of the grounds for a look at the world's largest cypress tree. Although it appears to be several trees growing together, it's actually one tree. The 100 foot tall colossus has a diameter exceeding thirty feet. They just don't come any bigger.

Parks and Camping

Azalea State Park

Location: Off Hwy 101, downtown Brookings
This delightful, tranquil day use park offers outstanding picnic sites that are encircled by azaleas of all sizes, some 20 feet high and over 300 years old. In late spring the azaleas are in bloom,

and the park explodes with the pastel colors and delicate fragrances of these flowering bushes. With a rich variety of shrubs, trees, paths, and glens, this small 36-acre park provides a natural area for kids to run, play, and explore in while the grown-ups kick off their shoes. A short trail leads up to a stone gazebo providing a breathtaking view of acres of azaleas and nicely landscaped gardens. On Memorial Day weekend the Azalea Festival (see description in this chapter) is held here.

Harris Beach State Park

Location: Off Hwy 101, 1 mile north of Brookings
Phone: 469–2021
Cost: Free/day use, $9–13/camping

Find the most alluring picture postcard you can, add a scenic day use area and a cozy campground with 151 sites (85 full or partial hookups), and you'll have Harris Beach State Park. Besides picture postcard views, the park offers sandy beaches, a rugged coastline, dense forests, and luxuriant underbrush. Harris, with its driftwood and boulder-strewn beaches, is a beachcomber's dream come true. Have an early breakfast, bundle up the youngsters and head down to the beach to watch the waves crash through the tunnels in the massive offshore rocks. These solitary rock spires, some 150 feet high, are constantly under attack from the surging sea. Imaginative youngsters will see why these sculptured rocks have led to names such as "Whales-head," "Hunchback," and "House Rock."

On most mornings a curious event unfolds offshore. If you can get out early enough, hike up to one of the higher points in the park and look out to sea. Right before your eyes a small fleet of commercial and sport fishing boats will congregate. Minutes later, the fleet will grow larger as other ships add on. In a short time, the small fleet has quadrupled in size to become an armada of hundreds of ships bobbing in the wave tossed sea.

Loeb State Park

Location: On North Bank Rd., 8 miles northeast of Brookings
Phone: 469–2021
Cost: Free/day use, $9–13/camping

Nestled in one of the largest old growth stands of rare myrtlewood, Loeb State Park offers day users restrooms and picnic sites, as well as 53 campsites with partial hookups for overnighters. With the Chetco River alongside, the park offers an attractive array of water recreation opportunities. On most summer days, the clear, warm waters of the Chetco prove irresistible to young swimmers, canoers, rafters, and inner tube drifters. Also within the park is a grove of towering redwoods replete with dark, shadowy trails and secret places that youngsters love to explore. Though you wouldn't want to go too far with young kids in tow, take one of the park's trails a bit into Oregon's largest and least-visited untamed areas— the Kalmiopsis Wilderness. You'll be treated to exotic plants, lush forests, and wildlife sightings. It's like a trip back in time.

Samuel Boardman State Park

Location: On Hwy 101, starts 3 miles north of Brookings

Boardman is a long, thin state park that stretches northward along Highway 101 providing some of the best vistas to be found anywhere on the entire Oregon Coast. Eleven viewpoints have been cut into the shoulder of Highway 101, providing motorists with safe sightseeing stops. Several of these have short trails down to the beach making perfect leg stretchers for young travellers. Indian Sands Trail is one of the more popular ones, meandering through thick underbrush and wind-dwarfed spruce to a bluff-top sand dune. Long ago, Indians gathered here to catch shellfish and make arrowheads. Even today, youngsters can enjoy the thrill of finding whole arrowheads among the piles of shells and flint chips.

The state park also features three sites that have picnic and restroom facilities, as well as short trails to the beach: Lone Ranch, Whale's Head, and Arch Rock. These are great spots for family outings, especially for imaginative children who will be captivated by the sights of ocean-carved monoliths reposing offshore.

Annual Events

Azalea Festival

Location: Azalea State Park on Park Rd., off Hwy 101, Brookings
Date: Memorial Day weekend
Phone: 469–3181

Brookings' biggest annual gala event is its Azalea Festival, which has been held each Memorial Day weekend since 1939. There's enough to see and do to occupy every member of the family the entire weekend. The fun begins with an enchanting flower float parade honoring the festival queen and her court. This dazzling floral fantasia is unforgettable. Among the other activities are a crafts fair with demonstrations, roving clowns and musicians, a five-kilometer run, an antique car display, kite flying demonstrations, and a seafood luncheon and beef barbecue. The setting for these festivities is a beautiful state park adorned with thousands of azaleas at the height of their bloom.

Beachcomber's Festival

Location: Call for beach locations
Date: Mid-March
Phone: 469–3181

Each year, tons of wood washes downstream and out to sea from logged forests throughout Oregon. Eventually, ocean waves return these assorted pieces of timber to the beaches as driftwood. It was only natural for a community to want to celebrate this glut of natural treasures. The annual Beachcomber's Festival does just that, featuring carved driftwood exhibits, slide shows, contests, and displays. Of special interest are the many craftspeople demonstrating their talents in creating unusual artworks from driftwood, agates, and other beachcombing discoveries. Children are fascinated to learn that some of these chunks of ash, oak, maple, myrtle, and redwood have spent decades at sea before being washed ashore.

Appendix

Oregon Coast Visitor Information Centers and Chambers of Commerce

Astoria Area Chamber of Commerce
111 W. Marine Dr.
P.O. Box 176
Astoria, OR 97103-0176
(503) 325-6311

Bandon Chamber of Commerce
300 S.E. 2nd
P.O. Box 1515
Bandon, OR 97411
(503) 347-9616

Bay Area Chamber of Commerce
50 E. Central Ave.
P.O. Box 210
Coos Bay, OR 97420
(800) 824-8486 or (503) 269-0215

Brookings-Harbor Chamber of Commerce
16255 Hwy 101
P.O. Box 940
Brookings, OR 97415
(503) 469-3181

Cannon Beach Chamber of Commerce
2nd and Spruce
P.O. Box 64
Cannon Beach, OR 97110
(503) 436-2623

Charleston Visitors Information Center
Boat Basin Dr. & Cape Arago Hwy
P.O. Box 5735
Charleston, OR 97420
(800) 824-8486 or (503) 888-2311

Depoe Bay Chamber of Commerce
663 S.E. Hwy 101
P.O. Box 21
Depoe Bay, Or 97341
(503) 765-2889

Florence Area Chamber of Commerce
270 Hwy 101
P.O. Box 26000
Florence, OR 97439
(503) 997-3128

Garibaldi Chamber of Commerce
P.O. Box 5
Garibaldi, OR 97118
(503) 322-0301

Gold Beach Chamber of Commerce
510 S. Ellenburg
P.O. Box 55
Gold Beach, OR 97444
(800) 525-2334 or (503) 247-7526

Lincoln City Chamber of Commerce
3939 N.W. Hwy 101
P.O. Box 787
Lincoln City, OR 97367
(800) 452-2151 or (503) 994-3070

Lower Umpqua Chamber of Commerce
Hwy 101 & Hwy 38
P.O. Box 11
Reedsport, OR 97467
(800) 247-2155 or (503) 271-3495

Nehalem Bay Area Chamber of Commerce
P.O. Box 238
Wheeler, OR 97147
(503) 368-5100

North Bend Information Center
Hwy 101, south end of McCullough Bridge
P.O. Box B
North Bend, OR 97459
(800) 824-8486 or (503) 756-4613

Greater Newport Chamber of Commerce
555 S.W. Coast Hwy
Newport, OR 97365
(800) 262-7844 or (503) 265-8801

Pacific City Woods Chamber of Commerce
P.O. Box 331
Pacific City, OR 97135
(503) 965-6161

Port Orford Chamber of Commerce
Between Jackson & Washington on Hwy 101
P.O. Box 637
Port Orford, OR 97465
(503) 332-8055

Rockaway Beach Chamber of Commerce
480 S. Hwy 101
P.O. Box 198
Rockaway Beach, OR 97136
(503) 355-8108

Seaside Chamber of Commerce
7 N. Roosevelt
P.O. Box 7
Seaside, OR 97138-6740
(800) 444-6740 or (503) 738-6391

Tillamook Chamber of Commerce
3705 Hwy 101 N.
Tillamook, OR 97141
(503) 842-7525

Waldport Chamber of Commerce
Hwy 101, south end of Alsea Bay Bridge
P.O. Box 669
Waldport, OR 97394
(503) 563-2133

Yachats Chamber of Commerce
441 Hwy 101
P.O. Box 174
Yachats, OR 97498
(503) 547-3530

Selected Reference Books

Brewster, David and Irving, Stephanie
Northwest Best Places
Seattle:Sasquatch Books, 1991

Bridges, Fraser
Pacific Coast Adventures
Vancouver, B.C.: Western Traveller Press, 1991

Canniff, Kiki
A Camper's Guide to Oregon and Washington
Portland: Kiki Enterprises, 1991

Canniff, Kiki
Free Campgrounds of Washington and Oregon
Portland: Kiki Enterprises, 1991

Craig, Darren and Julie
The Festival Hopper's Guide To The Great Northwest
San Jose, CA: Creative Chaos, 1991

Deaton, Carolyn
Best Choices On The Oregon Coast
Eugene: Global Publishing, 1991

Demaree, Tom
The Menu: A Restaurant Guide to Oregon
Hillsboro: David Thomas Publishing, 1991

Ferguson, Gary
Walks of The Pacific Northwest
New York: Prentice Hall Press, 1991

Friedman, Ralph
In Search of Western Oregon
Caldwell, ID: The Caxton Printers, LTD, 1990

Gousha, H.M.
Pacific Northwest Road Atlas and Visitor's Guide
New York: Simon and Schuster, 1992

Gulick, Bill
Roadside History of Oregon
Missoula, MT: Mountain Press Publishing Co., 1991

Harris, Richard
2 to 22 Days In The Pacific Northwest
Santa Fe, NM: John Muir Publications, 1992

Henderson, Bonnie
Best Hikes With Children in Western and Central Oregon
Seattle: The Mountaineers, 1992

Hoffman, Alison (Editor)
Fodor's 92 Pacific Northwest Coast
New York: Fodor's Travel Publications, 1992

Holman, Wendy and Nolan, Sheila
Where to Stay and Play Along the Pacific Coast
Seattle: N.W. Beachcomber Publishing, 1990

Hoy, Mark
Oregon Backroads
Helena, MT: American Geographic Publishing, 1988

Lampman, Linda, and Wiecks, Carolyn
The Portland Guidebook
Seattle: JASI Publishers, 1989

McFarlane, Marilyn
Quick Escapes in The Pacific Northwest
Chester, CT: The Globe Pequot Press, 1991

Metzler, Ken
The Best of Oregon
Portland: Timber Press, 1986

Oakley, Myrna
Oregon Off The Beaten Path
Chester, CT: The Globe Pequot Press, 1991

Oberrecht, Kenn
Driving The Pacific Coast
Chester, CT: The Globe Pequot Press, 1991

Olmsted, Gerald
The Best of The Pacific Coast
New York: Crown Publishers, 1989

American Automobile Association
Oregon Washington Tour Book
Heathrow, FL: American Automobile Association
(AAA), 1991

Preston, Thomas and Elizabeth
Western State Parks, Vol. 1, Pacific Northwest
Billings, MT: Discovery Publishing, 1991

Schultz, Steward T.
The Northwest Coast
Portland: Timber Press, 1990

Sunset
Sunset Oregon Travel Guide
Menlo Park, CA: Lane Publishing Co., 1987

Thoele, Mike
Footprints Across Oregon
Portland: Graphic Arts Center Publishing Co., 1991

Tuttle, Craig and Wanner, Linda
Beautiful America's Oregon Coast
Wilsonville: Beautiful America Publishing Co., 1991

Warren, Stuart and Ishikawa, Ted
Oregon Handbook
Chico, CA: Moon Publications, 1991

Whitmire, Tim (Editor)
Let's Go 1992: The Budget Guide To The Pacific Northwest, Western Canada and Alaska
New York: St. Martin's Press, 1992

Wood, Amos
Beachcombing The Pacific
West Chester, PA: Schiffer Publishing, 1987

Index

Index of Special Subjects

About the Authors

Carolyn Gabbe has worked in advertising, co-owned two retail gift stores in California and Oregon, and co-authored The Portland Super Shopper, a guidebook to Portland's hottest shopping bargains. She has lived in San Diego, Los Angeles, and Portland, and travelled throughout North America and Europe. Since their two children were toddlers, Carolyn and David have travelled extensively along the coasts of California, Oregon and Washington.

David Gabbe, a former investigator with the IRS and U.S. Labor Department, is the author of Wage and Hour Law Compliance Made Simple and co-author of The Portland Super Shopper. He has been a contributor to newspapers and magazines on a wide range of issues, including taxation, labor laws, nutrition, and political satire. He has travelled on three continents, and now makes his home in Eugene, Oregon, with his wife, Carolyn, and children, C.J. and Wendy.